NO GALLBLADDER

DIET COOKBOOK

Over 2000 Days of Tasty and Easy-to-Digest Recipes |
Comprehensive 28-Day Meal Plan for a Smooth
Recovery Post-Surgery

Salena Ryan

D1716853

TABLE OF CONTENTS

CHAPTER 1: UNDERSTANDING LIFE WITHOUT A GALLBLADDER

1.1 THE ROLE OF THE GALLBLADDER IN DIGESTION

Imagine your gallbladder as a tiny but crucial storage tank, nestled under your liver, playing a vital backstage role in the grand production of digestion. Despite its modest size, its functions are both intricate and essential, harmonizing with the liver to manage and optimize the digestion of fats.

Your liver is constantly producing bile, a complex fluid essential for breaking down dietary fats. However, this bile is not immediately required in large quantities all the time. Here's where the gallbladder steps in. Acting as a reservoir, the gallbladder stores bile produced by the liver, concentrating it by removing excess water, making it more potent. Think of this process as akin to brewing a strong cup of tea – more concentrated and effective for its purpose.

When you eat a meal, especially one rich in fats, your digestive system springs into action. The presence of fats in your small intestine signals the release of a hormone called cholecystokinin (CCK). This hormone prompts the gallbladder to contract and release its concentrated bile through the bile ducts into the small intestine. This timely release ensures that bile is available precisely when fats need to be emulsified – a process akin to how dish soap breaks down grease, making it easier to wash away.

This emulsification is critical because it transforms large fat molecules into smaller droplets, increasing their surface area and making them more accessible to digestive enzymes like lipase. Without this process, fats would remain in large globules, much harder for the body to digest and absorb. The bile also helps in the absorption of fat-soluble vitamins such as A, D, E, and K, ensuring that these essential nutrients can be efficiently utilized by the body.

In essence, the gallbladder functions as both a storage facility and a manager of bile, coordinating its release to match the body's digestive needs. By concentrating and timing the release of bile, the gallbladder ensures that your digestive system operates smoothly and efficiently, making the process of fat digestion as seamless as possible.

Understanding this nuanced role of the gallbladder highlights why its removal necessitates dietary adjustments. Without this vital organ, bile is released continuously but less effectively, necessitating a more mindful approach to fat consumption. Appreciating the gallbladder's function allows you to adapt to its absence with informed and thoughtful dietary choices, maintaining digestive health and comfort.

How the Gallbladder Functions

The gallbladder, a small pear-shaped organ nestled beneath the liver, plays a vital role in our digestive system, quietly orchestrating the breakdown of fats with remarkable efficiency. To understand how the gallbladder functions is to appreciate its elegance and precision in the complex symphony of digestion.

Your liver, a diligent and unceasing worker, continuously produces bile – a greenish-brown fluid essential for digesting fats. However, this bile is not needed all the time. The gallbladder acts as a storage unit, collecting and concentrating bile until it's called into action. Picture this: the gallbladder carefully removes water from the bile, making it a powerful concentrate, much like reducing a sauce to intensify its flavor.

When you eat a meal, especially one rich in fats, your digestive system sends a signal via a hormone called cholecystokinin (CCK). This hormone prompts the gallbladder to contract, pushing the concentrated bile through a network of ducts into the small intestine. This process is perfectly timed to ensure that bile meets the fats right when they need emulsifying. Imagine adding soap to greasy water – the bile breaks down fat molecules into smaller droplets, making them easier to digest.

The emulsification process facilitated by bile is crucial. It increases the surface area of fat droplets, allowing digestive enzymes to break them down more effectively. Without bile's detergent-like action, fats would remain large, indigestible globules. This efficient breakdown enables the body to absorb fats and fat-soluble vitamins like A, D, E, and K, which are essential for various bodily functions, from vision to immune response.

In essence, the gallbladder functions as a sophisticated manager of bile, ensuring it is available in the right quantity and potency precisely when needed. It stores and concentrates bile, then releases it in response to dietary fats, seamlessly integrating its activity with the overall digestive process.

However, life without a gallbladder requires the body to adapt. Without this storage and timing mechanism, bile flows continuously into the small intestine in a diluted form, which can be less effective at breaking down large amounts of fat at once. This continuous trickle necessitates dietary adjustments, emphasizing smaller, more frequent meals that are lower in fat.

Understanding the gallbladder's role highlights the importance of adapting to its absence. By appreciating how the gallbladder functions, you can make informed dietary choices that support your digestive health, ensuring that you continue to thrive even without this small but significant organ.

Changes in Digestion Post-Surgery

Adjusting to life without a gallbladder can be a significant change, especially when it comes to digestion. Post-surgery, your digestive system needs to adapt to the absence of this small but vital organ. Understanding these changes can help you navigate your new dietary landscape with confidence and ease.

When the gallbladder is removed, bile flows directly from the liver into the small intestine, rather than being stored and concentrated. This continuous trickle of bile can make it harder for your body to digest large amounts of fat at once, leading to common symptoms like diarrhea, bloating, and indigestion. However, these issues can be managed with some adjustments to your diet and eating habits.

One of the most noticeable changes after surgery is the need to follow a low-fat diet. Since the gallbladder is no longer there to release concentrated bile to break down fats, eating smaller, low-fat meals can help your digestive system process food more effectively. Focus on incorporating lean proteins, whole grains, and plenty of fruits and vegetables into your meals. Avoiding fried foods, fatty cuts of meat, and full-fat dairy products can also make a significant difference in how you feel after eating.

Another adjustment is the importance of eating smaller, more frequent meals throughout the day. Large meals can overwhelm your digestive system, leading to discomfort and other symptoms. By eating smaller portions more often, you can help your body manage the continuous flow of bile and improve nutrient absorption. This approach also helps maintain steady energy levels and prevents the hunger that often leads to poor food choices.

Fiber becomes your friend in this new dietary regime. Incorporating high-fiber foods such as oats, beans, and vegetables can aid digestion and help regulate bowel movements. However, it's important to increase fiber intake gradually to avoid gas and bloating. Drinking plenty of water is equally crucial, as it helps fiber move smoothly through your digestive system and prevents constipation.

Additionally, staying mindful of potential trigger foods is essential. While everyone's digestive system reacts differently, some common culprits include caffeine, spicy foods, and carbonated beverages. Keeping a food diary can help identify specific foods that may cause discomfort, allowing you to adjust your diet accordingly.

Adapting to these changes might feel overwhelming at first, but with time, you'll find a balance that works for you. The journey to optimal digestive health without a gallbladder is unique for each individual, but armed with knowledge and a willingness to experiment, you can discover a diet that supports your well-being and allows you to enjoy food without discomfort. Remember, patience and listening to your body are key to a smooth transition and long-term digestive health.

Common Symptoms and How to Manage Them

Living without a gallbladder brings its own set of challenges, particularly when it comes to managing common symptoms. For many, the journey post-surgery can feel like navigating uncharted waters, but understanding what to expect and how to address these symptoms can make the transition smoother.

One of the most common issues you might face is diarrhea. Without the gallbladder's-controlled release of bile, bile continuously drips into your intestines, which can lead to lose stools. This can be particularly frustrating, but there are ways to manage it. First, focusing on a low-fat diet can help significantly. High-fat foods tend to trigger more bile production, exacerbating diarrhea. Instead, opt for lean proteins, whole grains, and plenty of fiber-rich fruits and vegetables. Fiber, particularly soluble fiber found in foods like oats and apples, can help solidify your stools.

Bloating and gas are other frequent complaints. These symptoms often arise because your body is adjusting to a new way of processing fats and digesting food. Smaller, more frequent meals can alleviate this discomfort by reducing the strain on your digestive system. Chewing your food thoroughly and eating slowly also helps, as it reduces the amount of air swallowed and gives your digestive tract a head starts in breaking down food.

Indigestion, or a feeling of fullness and discomfort after eating, is another symptom many experience. This can be managed by avoiding foods known to cause indigestion, such as spicy dishes, caffeine, and carbonated beverages. Keeping a food diary can be incredibly beneficial in identifying specific triggers that might be unique to you. Additionally, staying upright for at least an hour after meals can help prevent indigestion by allowing gravity to aid the digestive process.

Nausea can occasionally occur, particularly if your body is struggling to digest certain foods. When nausea strikes, ginger tea or peppermint can be soothing. It's also crucial to stay hydrated, as dehydration can worsen nausea. Sipping water throughout the day and avoiding large amounts of liquid during meals can keep your hydration levels steady without overwhelming your stomach.

Adapting to these changes involves patience and a bit of trial and error. Each person's body reacts differently to the absence of a gallbladder, so what works for one might not work for another. Listening to your body, making gradual dietary adjustments, and staying mindful of your symptoms are key strategies in managing life without a gallbladder. Over time, with careful attention and self-care, you'll find a routine that works for you, allowing you to enjoy meals and maintain digestive comfort.

1.2 COMMON CHALLENGES AFTER GALLBLADDER REMOVAL

The journey after gallbladder removal is often accompanied by a series of common challenges. Understanding and addressing these hurdles can make the recovery process smoother and more manageable.

One of the primary challenges is adjusting to dietary changes. The gallbladder plays a crucial role in fat digestion, and without it, your body needs to adapt to a different way of processing fats. This often means adopting a low-fat diet, which can initially feel restrictive. However, this adjustment is essential for minimizing digestive discomfort. Focusing on lean proteins, whole grains, and a variety of fruits and vegetables can help ease this transition. Over time, you'll discover new, delicious ways to enjoy meals that align with your body's needs.

Digestive issues such as diarrhea, bloating, and gas are also common. These symptoms can be particularly challenging in the early weeks post-surgery. It's important to remember that your digestive system is learning to function without the gallbladder's bile regulation. Eating smaller, more frequent meals can alleviate these symptoms by preventing your digestive system from becoming overwhelmed. Additionally, incorporating soluble fiber into your diet can help manage diarrhea, while avoiding gas-producing foods like beans and carbonated drinks can reduce bloating.

Emotional and psychological adjustments are another significant aspect of life post-surgery. It's not uncommon to feel frustrated or anxious about the changes in your body and diet. The fear of experiencing digestive discomfort can sometimes overshadow the joy of eating. Acknowledging these feelings and giving yourself grace during this transition is crucial. Support groups, whether in-person or online, can provide a sense of community and reassurance that you are not alone in this journey.

Navigating social situations and eating out can also pose challenges. It might feel daunting to explain your dietary restrictions to friends and family, or to find suitable options at restaurants. Planning ahead can ease these worries. Look up menus online before dining out, and don't hesitate to ask for modifications to suit your dietary needs. Most establishments are willing to accommodate special requests, and having a plan can help you feel more confident and in control.

Each person's experience after gallbladder removal is unique, and the path to finding a new normal involves patience and experimentation. By staying informed, seeking support, and being proactive about your health, you can overcome these challenges and embrace a fulfilling, digestive-friendly lifestyle.

Digestive Issues and Solutions

After gallbladder removal, digestive issues can become a common part of daily life, but understanding these challenges and finding practical solutions can help you regain control and comfort.

Diarrhea is a frequent complaint, often caused by the constant drip of bile into the intestines. This can be particularly distressing, but several strategies can help manage it. First, adopting a low-fat diet can significantly reduce diarrhea. High-fat foods stimulate bile production, which can exacerbate the issue. Instead, focus on lean proteins, whole grains, and fiber-rich foods. Soluble fiber, found in oats, apples, and carrots, can help firm up stools and ease diarrhea. Additionally, staying hydrated is crucial, as diarrhea can lead to dehydration. Drinking plenty of water throughout the day helps maintain fluid balance and supports overall digestive health.

Bloating and gas are also common after gallbladder removal. These symptoms occur as your digestive system adapts to processing food without the gallbladder's bile regulation. To minimize bloating, consider eating smaller, more frequent meals. This approach helps prevent your digestive system from becoming overwhelmed and reduces the likelihood of gas buildup. Avoiding foods known to cause gas, such as beans, cabbage, and carbonated beverages, can also help. Incorporating probiotics into your diet, through foods like yogurt or supplements, can promote a healthy balance of gut bacteria and alleviate bloating.

Indigestion, characterized by discomfort or a feeling of fullness after eating, is another issue many face. This can be managed by avoiding trigger foods such as spicy dishes, caffeine, and fatty meals. Chewing food thoroughly and eating slowly can aid digestion and reduce the risk of indigestion. If you experience persistent indigestion, keeping a food diary can help identify specific triggers, allowing you to adjust your diet accordingly.

Nausea, though less common, can also be a problem. When nausea strikes, ginger tea or peppermint can provide relief. Eating bland, easily digestible foods, such as bananas, rice, applesauce, and toast, can soothe the stomach. It's also beneficial to avoid lying down immediately after eating, as this can exacerbate nausea.

Navigating these digestive issues requires patience and attentiveness to your body's signals. By making mindful dietary choices and adopting healthy eating habits, you can manage these symptoms effectively and enjoy a better quality of life post-surgery. Remember, each person's experience is unique, and finding what works best for you may take some time. With persistence and care, you can achieve a balanced and comfortable digestive routine.

Navigating Dietary Restrictions

Adjusting to dietary restrictions after gallbladder removal can feel like stepping into a whole new world. The foods you once enjoyed without a second thought might now cause discomfort, and navigating these changes can be daunting. However, with a bit of guidance and a positive outlook, you can find a new rhythm that supports your health and well-being.

The primary dietary restriction you'll face is fat intake. Without a gallbladder to regulate bile release, high-fat foods can be particularly troublesome, often leading to indigestion or diarrhea. To mitigate these issues, it's essential to focus on a low-fat diet. This doesn't mean sacrificing flavor or satisfaction; rather, it encourages a shift towards healthier, more balanced meals. Opt for lean proteins like chicken, turkey, and fish. Embrace the abundance of fruits and vegetables, which not only support digestion but also offer a rainbow of nutrients. Whole grains like brown rice, quinoa, and whole wheat bread should become staples in your pantry.

Another common restriction involves avoiding certain foods that can trigger digestive distress. Spicy foods, caffeine, and carbonated beverages are often culprits. While it might be challenging to cut out your morning coffee or favorite spicy dish, there are delicious alternatives. Herbal teas can replace coffee, offering a soothing start to your day. Mild herbs and spices like basil, oregano, and turmeric can add flavor without the heat.

Eating smaller, more frequent meals is another strategy to navigate dietary restrictions. Large meals can overwhelm your digestive system, especially in the absence of the gallbladder's bile regulation. By consuming smaller portions throughout the day, you help your body manage bile flow more effectively. This approach not only reduces the risk of discomfort but also helps maintain steady energy levels.

Social situations and eating out can pose additional challenges. It's helpful to plan ahead, checking restaurant menus for suitable options or suggesting places that offer healthier choices. Don't hesitate to ask for modifications; most restaurants are happy to accommodate dietary needs. For instance, you can request grilled instead of fried foods or ask for dressings and sauces on the side.

Remember, adapting to these restrictions is a journey. There will be trial and error, and that's perfectly okay. Listen to your body and be patient with yourself. Over time, you'll develop a new normal that supports your digestive health without compromising on taste and enjoyment. With each small adjustment, you are paving the way to a healthier, more comfortable lifestyle post-surgery.

Emotional and Psychological Adjustments

Adjusting to life after gallbladder removal isn't just a physical journey; it's an emotional and psychological one too. Many people find themselves grappling with a range of feelings, from relief and hope to frustration and anxiety. Understanding these emotional shifts and finding ways to cope can make this transition smoother and more manageable.

One of the first emotional hurdles is accepting the permanent change to your body. The gallbladder, though small, plays a significant role in digestion. Its absence can leave you feeling vulnerable and concerned about your digestive health. It's important to allow yourself to grieve this loss and acknowledge that it's normal to feel apprehensive. Embracing this new reality involves patience and self-compassion. Remind yourself that adapting to these changes takes time, and it's okay to feel uncertain along the way.

The psychological impact of dietary restrictions can also be challenging. Food is deeply intertwined with our social lives, traditions, and personal pleasures. Suddenly having to modify your diet can feel like a loss of control and enjoyment. To combat this, focus on what you can eat and explore new foods and recipes that fit within your dietary needs. This can be an opportunity to discover delicious, healthy options that you might not have tried otherwise. Sharing these new meals with friends and family can help you feel more connected and less isolated in your journey.

Anxiety about potential digestive issues is another common psychological adjustment. The fear of experiencing discomfort after eating can overshadow the joy of meals and social gatherings. One way to manage this anxiety is by keeping a food diary to track what foods you tolerate well and which ones cause issues. Over time, this can help you feel more confident in your food choices and reduce anxiety. Mindfulness practices, such as deep breathing and meditation, can also be beneficial in managing stress and promoting a sense of calm.

Seeking support from others who have gone through similar experiences can be incredibly comforting. Whether through in-person support groups or online communities, connecting with others who understand your challenges can provide reassurance and practical advice. Sharing your journey and hearing others' stories can help you feel less alone and more empowered to navigate life without a gallbladder.

Ultimately, the emotional and psychological adjustments after gallbladder removal are as important as the physical ones. By acknowledging your feelings, seeking support, and embracing new dietary habits, you can find a balance that supports both your mental and physical well-being. This journey is unique for everyone, but with time and self-care, you can achieve a fulfilling and healthy life post-surgery.

1.3 ADAPTING TO A NEW DIET: WHAT TO EXPECT

Adjusting to a new diet after gallbladder removal can be both a challenge and an opportunity. Understanding what to expect can help ease this transition and set you on a path toward healthier eating habits that support your digestion and overall well-being.

In the first few week's post-surgery, your body will be getting used to functioning without a gallbladder. This is a time for gentle, careful eating. You might find that smaller, more frequent meals are easier on your digestive system than larger ones. This approach helps to avoid overwhelming your digestive tract with too much fat at once, which can cause discomfort or diarrhea. Think of this period as a chance to reset your eating habits, focusing on balanced, nutrient-dense foods that are easy to digest.

As you move beyond the initial recovery phase, you'll begin to discover what foods work best for your new digestive system. Lean proteins, such as chicken, turkey, and fish, will likely become staples in your diet. These provide essential nutrients without the high fat content that can be problematic. Incorporate plenty of fiber-rich fruits and vegetables, which not only aid digestion but also contribute to overall health. Whole grains, like brown rice, quinoa, and whole wheat bread, are excellent sources of energy that are kind to your digestive system.

It's also important to stay hydrated. Drinking plenty of water aids digestion and helps your body process fiber more effectively. Herbal teas, particularly those with ginger or peppermint, can soothe your digestive system and provide additional hydration.

Expect some trial and error as you adapt to your new diet. Keeping a food diary can be immensely helpful in tracking what works well for you and what doesn't. This practice allows you to identify any foods that trigger discomfort and adjust your diet accordingly.

Social situations and dining out may require a bit more planning, but they are entirely manageable. Look up menus in advance and don't hesitate to ask for modifications that suit your dietary needs. Most restaurants are accommodating and can prepare dishes with less fat or without certain ingredients.

Throughout this journey, be patient with yourself. Adapting to a new diet is a process, and it's okay to have setbacks. Each person's experience is unique, and finding what works for you might take some time. With persistence and a positive attitude, you'll develop a diet that supports your health and allows you to enjoy a variety of delicious, satisfying foods. This adjustment period is an opportunity to cultivate eating habits that will benefit you for years to come.

The first few weeks after gallbladder surgery are a crucial period of adjustment for your body. This time is marked by healing and learning how to navigate your new digestive landscape. Understanding what to expect can help you manage this transition smoothly and with confidence.

Immediately following surgery, your digestive system is in a delicate state. The removal of the gallbladder, which stored and concentrated bile, means that bile now flows directly from the liver into your small intestine. This can make digesting fats more challenging initially. To help your body adjust, it's wise to start with a bland, low-fat diet. Think of simple, easy-to-digest foods such as broths, plain rice, bananas, and applesauce. These foods are gentle on your system and can help prevent any undue strain on your digestion.

As you progress in your recovery, gradually reintroduce more solid foods. Pay close attention to how your body reacts to different foods. Smaller, more frequent meals can be beneficial during this period, as they are easier for your digestive system to handle. For instance, instead of three large meals, aim for five or six smaller ones throughout the day. This approach not only helps with digestion but also maintains steady energy levels.

Hydration is another key aspect of your recovery. Drinking plenty of water supports digestion and helps prevent constipation, a common issue post-surgery. Herbal teas, especially those with ginger or chamomile, can be soothing and beneficial for your digestive tract.

It's also normal to experience some discomfort or digestive issues like bloating, gas, or diarrhea during these initial weeks. These symptoms are typically temporary and should gradually improve as your body adapts. Keeping a food diary can be incredibly helpful. By noting what you eat and any symptoms you experience, you can identify specific triggers and adjust your diet accordingly.

Rest is crucial during this healing period, but light physical activity, such as short walks, can aid digestion and boost your overall recovery. Listen to your body and avoid strenuous activities until you're fully healed.

Emotionally, this period can be challenging as well. It's common to feel a mix of relief and anxiety about the changes in your body and diet. Lean on your support system—friends, family, or support groups—who can offer encouragement and practical advice.

Overall, the first few week's post-surgery are about gentle adjustments and patience. By nurturing your body with the right foods, staying hydrated, and allowing yourself time to heal, you set the foundation for a smoother, more comfortable transition to life without a gallbladder. This period is just the beginning of your journey towards finding a new balance and embracing a healthy, fulfilling diet.

As you settle into life without a gallbladder, long-term dietary adjustments become an essential part of your new routine. These adjustments are not about restrictive dieting but rather about discovering a balanced approach to eating that supports your digestive health and overall well-being.

One of the key adjustments is maintaining a low-fat diet. While you don't have to eliminate fats entirely, it's crucial to choose healthy fats and consume them in moderation. Focus on sources like avocados, nuts, seeds, and olive oil, which are easier for your body to process. Avoid high-fat and fried foods, as they can overwhelm your digestive system and cause discomfort. Lean proteins such as chicken, turkey, fish, and plant-based options like beans and lentils should form the foundation of your meals. These provide the necessary nutrients without the excess fat.

Fiber continues to play a vital role in your diet. It aids digestion and helps regulate bowel movements, which can be particularly beneficial as your body adjusts to its new bile flow. Incorporate a variety of fruits, vegetables, whole grains, and legumes into your meals. However, increase your fiber intake gradually to avoid gas and bloating, and always pair high-fiber foods with plenty of water to help them move smoothly through your digestive tract.

Staying hydrated is crucial for digestive health. Water helps in the digestion and absorption of nutrients and prevents constipation. Aim to drink at least eight glasses of water a day, and consider herbal teas, particularly those with digestive benefits like ginger or peppermint, as part of your hydration plan.

Mindful eating is another long-term adjustment that can make a significant difference. Take time to chew your food thoroughly and eat slowly. This not only aids in digestion but also helps you to enjoy your meals more and recognize when you are full, preventing overeating.

Understanding and identifying food triggers is an ongoing process. Keeping a food diary can help you pinpoint which foods consistently cause issues and which ones are well-tolerated. This knowledge allows you to make informed choices and avoid unnecessary discomfort.

Social situations and dining out require a bit of planning but are entirely manageable. Most restaurants offer healthier options, and many are willing to accommodate special dietary requests. Don't hesitate to ask for modifications, such as grilling instead of frying or serving sauces on the side. Being prepared and knowing your options can help you enjoy social meals without worry.

Finally, be patient with yourself. Adjusting to a new way of eating takes time, and it's natural to have occasional setbacks. Each person's journey is unique, and finding what works best for you may involve some trial and error. With persistence and a positive outlook, you'll establish a diet that supports your health and allows you to enjoy a variety of delicious foods.

Tips for Success

Navigating life after gallbladder removal can be a journey of discovery and adaptation. With a few practical tips, you can achieve success in managing your diet and maintaining digestive health. These strategies will help you transition smoothly and enjoy a fulfilling, balanced lifestyle.

First and foremost, listen to your body. Everyone's digestive system reacts differently to the absence of a gallbladder, so it's essential to pay attention to how specific foods make you feel. Keeping a food diary can be incredibly useful. By tracking what you eat and noting any symptoms, you can identify patterns and make informed decisions about your diet. This personal log becomes a valuable tool in understanding your unique digestive responses.

Another key tip is to embrace smaller, more frequent meals. Instead of the traditional three large meals a day, try eating five or six smaller portions. This approach helps your digestive system handle food more efficiently and prevents overwhelming it with too much at once. It also helps maintain steady energy levels throughout the day, keeping you feeling satisfied and nourished.

Hydration is vital for digestive health. Drinking plenty of water aids in the digestion and absorption of nutrients and helps prevent constipation. Aim for at least eight glasses of water a day, and consider integrating herbal teas like peppermint or ginger, which can soothe your digestive tract.

Incorporating fiber into your diet is another crucial step. Foods rich in soluble fiber, such as oats, apples, and carrots, can help regulate your digestive system and improve bowel movements. Remember to increase fiber intake gradually and drink plenty of water to avoid gas and bloating.

When dining out or attending social events, plan ahead. Look at menus online and choose restaurants that offer healthier, low-fat options. Don't hesitate to ask for modifications to your meal, such as grilling instead of frying or serving dressings on the side. Being proactive about your choices ensures you can enjoy social occasions without compromising your dietary needs.

Experimenting with different foods and cooking methods can also lead to success. Discovering new recipes and flavors keeps your diet interesting and enjoyable. You might find that certain cooking techniques, like steaming or baking, work better for your

CHAPTER 2: ESSENTIAL NUTRITIONAL GUIDELINES POST-SURGERY

2.1 IMPORTANCE OF A LOW-FAT DIET

The first few weeks after gallbladder removal can feel like uncharted territory. You might find yourself uncertain about what to eat, how your body will react, and whether you'll ever feel "normal" again. Rest assured, these concerns are common, and with a bit of patience and adaptation, you'll soon find a new rhythm.

Initially, your diet will need to be bland and simple. Your body is adjusting to the absence of the gallbladder, which used to help digest fats. Stick to low-fat foods and introduce them slowly. Think of plain rice, steamed vegetables, and lean proteins like chicken and fish. Small, frequent meals are more manageable than large ones, easing the digestive load and helping prevent discomfort.

As you progress into the long-term phase, you'll notice that your body starts to adjust. Gradually, you'll be able to reintroduce a wider variety of foods. However, it's crucial to keep your diet low in fat. High-fat foods can trigger digestive distress, leading to symptoms like bloating and diarrhea. Pay close attention to your body's responses and avoid foods that cause issues.

Success in adapting to this new diet hinges on a few key strategies. Planning your meals ahead of time can alleviate stress and ensure you always have suitable options available. Keep a well-stocked pantry with low-fat staples and invest in kitchen gadgets that make meal prep easier, like a slow cooker or a good blender. Experiment with herbs and spices to add flavor without adding fat.

Remember, every individual's response to dietary changes can differ. Be patient with yourself and give your body the time it needs to adapt. With thoughtful adjustments and a bit of culinary creativity, you can enjoy a diet that supports both your recovery and long-term health.

Embracing a low-fat diet after gallbladder surgery isn't just a temporary adjustment; it's a transformative approach to lifelong wellness. Reducing fat intake can have profound benefits, helping your body navigate its new digestive reality with ease.

Without a gallbladder, your body's ability to store and concentrate bile is diminished, which makes digesting fats more challenging. When you consume high-fat foods, your liver must produce bile on demand, which can lead to digestive distress. Symptoms like bloating, diarrhea, and abdominal pain can quickly follow a fatty meal. By opting for low-fat choices, you're not only minimizing these uncomfortable symptoms but also supporting a smoother digestive process.

Beyond immediate relief, reducing fat intake offers long-term health advantages. A diet lower in fat often means higher in fruits, vegetables, and whole grains – foods rich in essential nutrients and fiber. These foods are easier to digest and provide steady energy, helping you maintain a balanced diet that promotes overall health.

Lowering your fat intake can also play a crucial role in weight management. Since high-fat foods are calorie-dense, reducing them can help prevent unwanted weight gain, which is especially important after surgery. Maintaining a healthy weight reduces the strain on your digestive system and lowers the risk of developing other health issues such as heart disease and diabetes.

Furthermore, this dietary shift can have a ripple effect on your lifestyle. It encourages mindfulness about food choices and fosters healthier eating habits. You might find yourself exploring new ingredients and cooking methods, discovering flavors and dishes you never considered before.

In essence, reducing fat intake is about more than just avoiding discomfort. It's about embracing a healthier, more vibrant way of living. By making thoughtful, low-fat choices, you're paving the way for a more comfortable recovery and a lifetime of better health.

Navigating the world of low-fat foods can initially feel like deciphering a complex puzzle. However, with a bit of guidance, you can easily identify foods that align with your new dietary needs post-surgery. The key is to focus on whole, unprocessed foods that naturally contain less fat while providing ample nutrients.

Start with fruits and vegetables, your new best friends. These vibrant, nutrient-dense options are naturally low in fat and high in fiber, vitamins, and minerals. They not only support digestion but also add color and variety to your meals. Think crisp apples, juicy berries, leafy greens, and crunchy bell peppers. Incorporating a rainbow of produce ensures a range of nutrients and keeps your meals exciting.

Lean proteins are another cornerstone of a low-fat diet. Skinless chicken, turkey, and fish are excellent choices, providing the protein your body needs without the extra fat. Seafood, in particular, offers a double benefit – it's low in fat and rich in omega-3 fatty acids, which are heart-healthy and anti-inflammatory. Don't overlook plant-based proteins like beans, lentils, and tofu. They're not only low in fat but also packed with fiber and essential nutrients.

Whole grains also play a significant role in this dietary shift. Opt for brown rice, quinoa, and whole wheat pasta over their refined counterparts. These grains are higher in fiber and help regulate blood sugar levels, keeping you full and satisfied longer.

Dairy can be tricky, but there are plenty of low-fat or fat-free options available. Skim milk, low-fat yogurt, and reduced-fat cheese can be included in your diet in moderation. These provide the calcium and protein your body needs without the added fat.

Lastly, be mindful of cooking methods. Grilling, baking, steaming, and poaching are your go-to techniques for preparing low-fat meals. These methods require little to no added fat, preserving the natural flavors and nutrients of your food.

By focusing on these wholesome, low-fat options, you'll not only support your recovery but also enjoy a diverse and satisfying diet. The journey to discovering low-fat foods is an opportunity to explore new flavors and healthier ways of eating, setting a foundation for long-term wellness.

Cooking low-fat meals post-surgery can be both an art and a science, transforming simple ingredients into delicious, healthy dishes without the excess fat. The secret lies in choosing the right techniques that enhance flavor while keeping your meals light and digestible.

Grilling is a fantastic method for preparing meats and vegetables. It allows the natural flavors to shine through while letting excess fat drip away. Imagine the sizzle of a perfectly grilled chicken breast or the charred sweetness of bell peppers and zucchini. Using a marinade with herbs, citrus, and a touch of olive oil can infuse your food with vibrant flavors without adding unwanted fat.

Steaming is another excellent technique, particularly for vegetables and fish. It preserves the nutrients and natural flavors, offering a tender, juicy result. Picture a plate of steamed salmon, flaky and moist, served with a side of bright green broccoli. Adding a squeeze of lemon or a sprinkle of fresh herbs can elevate these simple dishes, making them both healthy and delightful.

Baking is a versatile technique that can be used for everything from proteins to vegetables. Baking allows for even cooking and can create a wonderful, caramelized crust without the need for excess oil. Think of a batch of root vegetables, slowly baked until golden and sweet, or a fillet of fish, baked with a medley of fresh herbs and a hint of garlic.

Stir-frying can also be a great option when done correctly. Using a small amount of oil and high heat, you can quickly cook vegetables and lean proteins, preserving their texture and flavor. Imagine a colorful stir-fry with snap peas, bell peppers, and strips of lean beef, all coming together in a harmonious blend of taste and nutrition.

Poaching is another gentle method, ideal for delicate proteins like fish and poultry. Cooking your food in a flavorful broth or seasoned water keeps it moist and tender. Visualize a poached chicken breast, infused with the subtle flavors of ginger and lemongrass, served alongside steamed jasmine rice.

Embracing these cooking techniques will help you create meals that are not only low in fat but also rich in flavor and nutrition. Experimenting with these methods can turn everyday ingredients into culinary delights, supporting your health and recovery with every bite.

Understanding which foods are safe and which are best avoided is crucial after gallbladder surgery. Your body now processes fats differently, and certain foods can either aid or hinder your digestion. Let's navigate this new culinary landscape together.

Imagine walking through a grocery store, your senses bombarded with an array of choices. The goal is to fill your cart with foods that will support your digestive health while steering clear of those that might cause discomfort. Fresh fruits and vegetables should be your first stop. Think of crisp apples, juicy berries, leafy greens, and crunchy carrots. These foods are low in fat and high in fiber, helping to keep your digestive system running smoothly.

Lean proteins are your allies in this new diet. Picture a succulent piece of grilled chicken, a tender fillet of fish, or a hearty portion of legumes like lentils and beans. These proteins provide essential nutrients without the fat content that can trigger digestive issues. Opt for plant-based proteins whenever possible; they offer the added benefit of fiber, which aids digestion.

Whole grains are another safe haven. Imagine a steaming bowl of brown rice, a slice of whole-grain bread, or a serving of quinoa. These grains are not only nutritious but also gentle on your digestive system. They provide steady energy and keep you feeling full longer, without the high fat content of processed grains.

Now, let's consider the foods to avoid. High-fat items like fried foods, fatty cuts of meat, and full-fat dairy products can be particularly problematic. Picture a greasy burger or a rich, creamy cheese; these might look tempting but can lead to bloating and discomfort. Processed snacks and sugary desserts are also best left on the shelf. These foods often contain hidden fats and sugars that can wreak havoc on your digestion.

Be cautious with certain vegetables and legumes as well. Cruciferous vegetables like broccoli and cauliflower, while healthy, can sometimes cause gas and bloating. It's all about balance and moderation.

By focusing on safe, nutritious options and being mindful of potential triggers, you'll find that navigating your new diet can be both manageable and enjoyable. Each meal becomes an opportunity to support your health and well-being, paving the way for a comfortable and vibrant life post-surgery.

After gallbladder surgery, knowing which foods to avoid is as important as knowing which ones to embrace. Certain foods can trigger discomfort and digestive issues, making it essential to steer clear of them to ensure a smooth recovery and ongoing well-being.

Picture a tempting platter of fried foods—crispy chicken wings, French fries, and onion rings. While these might have been occasional indulgences before, they are now best avoided. Fried foods are high in fat, which can be difficult for your body to process without a gallbladder, often leading to bloating, gas, and diarrhea.

Think about rich, fatty cuts of meat like bacon, sausages, and rib-eye steaks. These are loaded with saturated fats that can strain your digestive system, causing discomfort and potentially leading to more serious health issues over time. Opting for leaner cuts of meat or plant-based proteins can make a significant difference in how you feel.

Dairy products, especially full-fat versions like whole milk, cream, butter, and cheese, can also pose problems. Imagine a creamy cheese platter or a decadent slice of cheesecake. These high-fat dairy items can trigger digestive distress post-surgery. Choosing low-fat or non-dairy alternatives can help maintain digestive harmony.

Sugary snacks and desserts, though often irresistible, should be limited as well. Consider a table full of pastries, candies, and rich cakes. These items are not only high in sugar but often contain hidden fats that can upset your digestion. It's best to enjoy natural sweets like fruits to satisfy your cravings without the adverse effects.

Processed foods, with their hidden fats, sugars, and additives, are another category to be cautious of. Think of packaged snacks, frozen dinners, and fast food. These convenient options often come with a cost to your digestive health, making it crucial to read labels carefully and choose whole, unprocessed foods instead.

By consciously avoiding these high-fat, high-sugar, and highly processed foods, you can support your body's healing process and maintain a more comfortable and healthier lifestyle. This mindful approach to eating will help you navigate post-surgery life with greater ease and confidence, ensuring that every meal contributes positively to your well-being.

Navigating life without a gallbladder means making mindful food choices, but it doesn't mean sacrificing taste or satisfaction. Finding safe alternatives to previously enjoyed high-fat foods can lead to delicious discoveries and a healthier lifestyle.

Imagine swapping out your morning fry-up for a vibrant bowl of oatmeal topped with fresh berries and a drizzle of honey. Oatmeal is not only comforting but also packed with fiber, helping to keep your digestive system running smoothly. It's a heart-healthy choice that can be dressed up in countless ways to keep breakfast exciting.

For those who love the richness of dairy, consider alternatives like almond milk, coconut yogurt, or cashew cheese. These plant-based options are naturally lower in fat and often fortified with essential nutrients like calcium and vitamin D. Picture a creamy smoothie made with almond milk, bursting with flavors from fresh fruits and a hint of vanilla—both satisfying and easy on the stomach.

When it comes to protein, lean cuts of poultry and fish are excellent choices. Think of a perfectly grilled salmon fillet, seasoned with herbs and a squeeze of lemon, providing a flavorful yet light main course. Plant-based proteins like beans, lentils, and tofu are equally beneficial. Envision a hearty lentil stew, rich in texture and full of comforting spices, offering a nutritious and low-fat alternative to heavier meat dishes.

For snack time, instead of reaching for chips or pastries, consider fresh fruits, vegetables, and whole grain crackers. Imagine the crunch of a crisp apple, the sweetness of ripe berries, or the satisfying bite of a handful of baby carrots dipped in hummus. These snacks are not only tasty but also packed with vitamins, minerals, and fiber, making them perfect for maintaining energy levels throughout the day.

When baking, experiment with using applesauce or mashed bananas in place of butter or oil. These substitutions add natural sweetness and moisture to your baked goods, creating treats that are both delicious and digestible. Visualize a slice of banana bread, moist and fragrant, paired with a cup of herbal tea for a comforting afternoon break.

By exploring these safe alternatives, you can create meals that are not only friendly to your digestive system but also delightful to your taste buds. Embracing these changes opens up a world of culinary possibilities, ensuring that your journey to better health is both enjoyable and nourishing.

Crafting balanced meals post-gallbladder surgery is about combining nutrition with flavor, ensuring that each bite supports your health and recovery. Imagine your plate as a canvas, where vibrant colors and diverse textures come together to create a harmonious and satisfying meal.

Start with a foundation of lean proteins. Visualize a succulent piece of grilled chicken breast, a fillet of baked salmon, or a hearty serving of lentils. These proteins are essential for muscle repair and overall health, providing the building blocks your body needs to heal and thrive.

Next, add a generous portion of vegetables. Think of the bright, fresh greens of spinach and kale, the vivid reds and oranges of bell peppers and carrots, and the deep purples of eggplant. These vegetables are not only rich in vitamins and minerals but also packed with fiber, aiding in digestion and keeping you feeling full and energized.

Incorporate whole grains to round out your meal. Picture a serving of fluffy quinoa, a side of brown rice, or a slice of whole grain bread. These grains provide sustained energy and additional fiber, helping to regulate blood sugar levels and support digestive health.

Healthy fats are still necessary, but they should be chosen wisely. Imagine drizzling a little olive oil over your vegetables or adding a few slices of avocado to your salad. These fats are heart-healthy and easier to digest, offering essential fatty acids without overwhelming your system.

2.3 NUTRITIONAL SUPPLEMENTS AND HYDRATION

Ensuring your body receives the right nutrients and stays well-hydrated is crucial after gallbladder surgery. Nutritional supplements and proper hydration can significantly enhance your recovery and support long-term health.

Think of supplements as your nutritional safety net. While a balanced diet should provide most of the essential nutrients, there are times when supplements can fill in the gaps. For instance, after gallbladder removal, you might find it challenging to absorb certain vitamins, particularly fat-soluble ones like A, D, E, and K. A high-quality multivitamin can help bridge this gap, ensuring you get the necessary vitamins your body needs to function optimally.

Calcium and magnesium are also important. These minerals support bone health and muscle function, and their absorption can be affected post-surgery. Imagine taking a calcium supplement paired with vitamin D to enhance absorption, or incorporating magnesium into your routine to support muscle relaxation and overall well-being.

Probiotics are another valuable addition. These beneficial bacteria can aid digestion and promote a healthy gut flora, which is especially important as your digestive system adjusts. Picture a daily probiotic supplement working quietly to balance your gut environment, helping to alleviate symptoms like bloating and irregularity.

Hydration is equally vital. Imagine your body as a well-oiled machine, where water acts as the essential lubricant. Proper hydration supports digestion, nutrient absorption, and overall bodily functions. Drinking plenty of water throughout the day is key. Consider starting your morning with a glass of water, sipping throughout meals, and keeping a water bottle with you as a constant reminder.

Herbal teas can also be a soothing and hydrating option. Think of a warm cup of chamomile or peppermint tea, which can help with digestion and provide a comforting, hydrating experience. Avoid sugary drinks and excessive caffeine, as they can lead to dehydration and digestive discomfort.

By incorporating the right supplements and maintaining adequate hydration, you provide your body with the support it needs to heal and thrive. Each supplement and sip of water is a step towards a stronger, healthier you, making this part of your recovery journey as smooth and effective as possible.

When adapting to life without a gallbladder, the significance of essential vitamins and minerals becomes paramount. These nutrients play a critical role in maintaining overall health and aiding digestion, which can be particularly delicate post-surgery.

Imagine vitamins and minerals as the unsung heroes of your dietary regime. They don't just support your immune system or bone health—they're integral to helping your body adjust to its new way of processing food. For instance, Vitamin D, often dubbed the sunshine vitamin, is vital for calcium absorption, helping to maintain bone strength. Without a gallbladder, your body might struggle with fat absorption, making Vitamin D supplementation something to consider, especially if you're not getting enough sunlight.

Vitamin B12, another essential nutrient, plays a key role in nerve function and the production of DNA and red blood cells. Post-surgery, your body's ability to absorb this vitamin might be compromised, leading to fatigue or neurological issues. Ensuring you get enough B12, whether through diet or supplements, can make a world of difference in your energy levels and overall health.

Then there's magnesium, a mineral involved in over 300 biochemical reactions in the body, including muscle and nerve function, blood sugar control, and blood pressure regulation. Without sufficient magnesium, you might experience muscle cramps, irregular heartbeats, or even mood swings. Foods like leafy greens, nuts, and seeds are excellent sources of magnesium, and incorporating them into your meals can help maintain balance.

Calcium is another crucial mineral, especially if you're concerned about bone health. With potential changes in how your body absorbs fats and nutrients, ensuring you get enough calcium from dairy alternatives like fortified plant milks or leafy greens is essential.

Iron, too, demands attention. Iron deficiency can lead to anemia, causing fatigue and weakness. Lean meats, beans, and fortified cereals can boost your iron intake, ensuring your blood cells carry oxygen efficiently throughout your body.

Hydration is equally important. Staying well-hydrated aids digestion and nutrient absorption. Drinking plenty of water, herbal teas, and low-sugar beverages can help keep your system running smoothly.

Incorporating these essential vitamins and minerals into your diet is not just about preventing deficiencies—it's about empowering your body to thrive in its new state. By focusing on nutrient-rich foods and considering supplements where necessary, you're laying the foundation for a healthier, more resilient you.

Imagine your body as a finely tuned orchestra, with each section playing its part in perfect harmony. Now, picture hydration as the conductor, guiding every instrument to create a beautiful symphony. Staying hydrated is essential, especially after gallbladder surgery, where the body's needs can shift in surprising ways.

Water is the most fundamental component of life, making up about 60% of our body weight. It's involved in nearly every bodily function, from regulating temperature to lubricating joints and aiding digestion. After gallbladder removal, your body's ability to process fats and flush out toxins may be altered, making hydration even more crucial.

Think of water as the oil in a machine. Without it, the gears can't turn smoothly, and the machine grinds to a halt. When you're well-hydrated, your digestive system works more efficiently, helping to move food through your intestines and absorb nutrients effectively. This is particularly important post-surgery, as your body adjusts to a new way of digesting food without the bile storage provided by the gallbladder.

Furthermore, hydration helps to keep your liver—the organ now taking on a more direct role in bile production—functioning optimally. An adequately hydrated liver can produce bile more efficiently, aiding in the digestion of fats and preventing discomfort and indigestion.

On a more personal level, staying hydrated can significantly impact your daily energy levels and overall well-being. Dehydration can lead to fatigue, headaches, and difficulty concentrating, making it harder to stick to your new dietary plan and maintain a positive outlook on your recovery journey.

One simple yet effective way to ensure you're drinking enough is to carry a water bottle with you and take small sips throughout the day. Herbal teas and water-rich foods like cucumbers and watermelon can also contribute to your daily fluid intake, providing variety and additional nutrients.

In essence, water is your body's silent ally, working behind the scenes to keep everything running smoothly. By prioritizing hydration, you're giving yourself the best possible support for a healthy recovery and a vibrant, energetic life post-surgery.

Imagine embarking on a journey where your body's nutritional needs are like a map guiding you to a healthier, more balanced life post-gallbladder surgery. Supplements can act as your trusty compass, ensuring you stay on course even when dietary adjustments alone aren't quite enough.

One of the most significant changes post-surgery is how your body processes fats and nutrients. This is where supplements come in handy, bridging the gap between what you eat and what your body actually absorbs. For example, bile salts can be incredibly beneficial. Without a gallbladder, your liver releases bile directly into the intestines, but not always in the right amounts or at the right time. Supplementing with bile salts can aid in digesting fats more efficiently, reducing discomfort and enhancing nutrient absorption.

Another crucial supplement is a high-quality multivitamin. Think of it as a nutritional safety net, catching any essential vitamins and minerals that might slip through the cracks. A well-rounded multivitamin ensures you're getting enough Vitamin A, D, E, and K—fat-soluble vitamins that are often poorly absorbed without a gallbladder. These vitamins play vital roles in everything from immune function to bone health.

Probiotics are also worth considering. These beneficial bacteria help maintain a healthy gut flora, which is essential for digestion and overall health. They can alleviate common post-surgery issues like bloating and irregular bowel movements, making your digestive system more resilient and efficient.

Fish oil supplements are another excellent addition. Rich in omega-3 fatty acids, they support heart health and reduce inflammation. Since your body might struggle with fat absorption, a good fish oil supplement ensures you're still getting these essential fatty acids in a form that's easier to digest.

CHAPTER 3: SETTING UP YOUR POST-GALLBLADDER KITCHEN

3.1 MUST-HAVE PANTRY STAPLES

Picture your kitchen as a sanctuary of wellness, a place where the right ingredients not only nourish your body but also support your new dietary needs post-gallbladder surgery. Stocking your pantry with the right staples can make all the difference in maintaining a balanced, low-fat diet that's both delicious and gentle on your digestive system.

First and foremost, let's talk about whole grains. Think of brown rice, quinoa, and oats as your new best friends. These grains are not only high in fiber, helping to keep your digestion smooth and regular, but they also provide a steady release of energy, avoiding the spikes and crashes that refined grains can cause. Plus, their nutty flavors add a satisfying depth to your meals.

Lean proteins are another cornerstone of your pantry. Canned beans and lentils are incredibly versatile and can be used in everything from soups to salads. They're packed with protein and fiber, making them filling without being heavy on the fat. Additionally, canned tuna or salmon in water can be a quick and convenient source of lean protein, perfect for those busy days when you need something fast and nutritious.

Healthy fats are essential, even if your body processes them differently now. Olive oil and avocado oil should be your go-to cooking oils. They're rich in monounsaturated fats, which are easier to digest and beneficial for your heart. Keep a small bottle of each within easy reach for sautéing vegetables or dressing salads.

Speaking of vegetables, having a variety of canned or jarred options like tomatoes, artichokes, and olives can add flavor and nutrition to your dishes without the hassle of constant fresh produce shopping. They're great for quick meals and can elevate the simplest recipes with their rich flavors.

Herbs and spices are the secret weapons of a flavorful, low-fat diet. Stock up on dried basil, oregano, cumin, and turmeric to add depth to your cooking without relying on fats. Fresh garlic and ginger are also fantastic for adding a punch of flavor and have anti-inflammatory properties that can aid digestion.

Lastly, don't forget your emergency stash. Low-sodium broths, both vegetable and chicken, can form the base of countless meals, from hearty soups to grain dishes. They're a comforting staple that adds flavor without extra fat, making them indispensable in your post-gallbladder kitchen.

With these pantry staples, you're not just setting yourself up for success; you're crafting a culinary environment that makes healthy, digestible meals an effortless part of your everyday life. Each ingredient is a step towards embracing your new dietary journey with confidence and creativity.

When setting up your post-gallbladder kitchen, the essence of every meal lies in the right ingredients. These essentials aren't just about fulfilling nutritional needs—they're about creating delicious, digestible dishes that support your health and recovery.

Start with your foundation: lean proteins. Skinless chicken breast, turkey, and fish such as salmon and cod are not only low in fat but also rich in essential nutrients that aid muscle repair and overall health. They provide a hearty base for a variety of meals, ensuring you stay satisfied without overwhelming your digestive system.

Vegetables are your next crucial element. Think vibrant, colorful, and full of life—like a garden on your plate. Leafy greens such as spinach and kale are packed with vitamins and minerals, while cruciferous vegetables like broccoli and cauliflower offer fiber and phytonutrients. These vegetables are gentle on your digestive tract and can be prepared in myriad ways to keep your meals exciting and nutritious.

Whole grains, such as quinoa, brown rice, and barley, play a significant role in providing sustained energy. They are easy to prepare and versatile enough to pair with almost any dish, adding a satisfying texture and nutty flavor that complements lean proteins and vegetables beautifully.

Healthy fats are also essential, despite your new dietary considerations. Avocados, nuts, and seeds like chia and flaxseeds offer heart-healthy fats that support brain function and overall wellness. Using small amounts of olive oil or avocado oil in your cooking can enhance flavors while keeping your meals light and digestible.

Herbs and spices are the final touch that brings your meals to life. Fresh herbs like basil, cilantro, and parsley not only add vibrant flavors but also possess digestive benefits. Spices such as turmeric, cumin, and ginger offer anti-inflammatory properties, aiding in digestion and adding a depth of flavor that can transform simple dishes into gourmet experiences.

Incorporating these essential ingredients into your everyday cooking ensures that each meal is not only a source of nourishment but also a pleasure to eat. By focusing on lean proteins, vibrant vegetables, whole grains, healthy fats, and flavorful herbs and spices, you're creating a balanced, delicious, and supportive diet that aligns perfectly with your post-gallbladder needs. This approach helps you embrace your new lifestyle with confidence and culinary creativity, turning every meal into an opportunity for nourishment and enjoyment.

Imagine your pantry as the heart of your kitchen, a place where health and convenience come together to support your journey post-gallbladder surgery. Stocking it wisely is like building a solid foundation for a house—it ensures that you have everything you need to create delicious, nutritious meals with ease.

Start with the basics: whole grains. Brown rice, quinoa, and whole wheat pasta are pantry staples that offer fiber and sustained energy. These grains are versatile, easy to cook, and pair well with a variety of dishes, making them perfect for your new dietary needs.

Next, consider your protein sources. Canned beans and lentils are excellent choices. They're packed with protein and fiber, and they're incredibly convenient. Whether you're whipping up a quick salad or a hearty stew, these legumes provide a robust nutritional profile that supports digestion and overall health.

Healthy fats are also crucial. Keep a bottle of extra-virgin olive oil on hand for cooking and dressings. It's rich in monounsaturated fats, which are easier on your digestive system and beneficial for heart health. Similarly, a jar of natural nut butter, such as almond or peanut butter, can add healthy fats and protein to snacks and meals.

Don't forget about your flavor enhancers. Herbs and spices like oregano, basil, cumin, and turmeric can transform a simple dish into a culinary delight. Not only do they add depth and complexity to your meals, but many also offer digestive and anti-inflammatory benefits.

Having a variety of canned or jarred vegetables is also essential. Items like canned tomatoes, artichokes, and olives are not only convenient but also add a burst of flavor and nutrition to your meals. They can be lifesavers when fresh produce is running low.

Stocking low-sodium broths—both vegetable and chicken—is another wise move. These broths can serve as a base for soups, stews, and grains, infusing your dishes with rich flavor without the added fat.

Lastly, consider having some whole grain crackers and rice cakes for quick, easy snacks that are gentle on your digestive system. Paired with a bit of nut butter or a slice of lean turkey, they can keep you satisfied between meals without overloading your system.

By thoughtfully stocking your pantry with these essentials, you create a kitchen that not only meets your post-gallbladder dietary needs but also inspires you to explore and enjoy a wide range of healthy, flavorful meals. This foundation helps you navigate your new culinary landscape with confidence and creativity, ensuring every meal is a step towards better health.

Navigating the world of grocery shopping on a budget can be daunting, especially when you're adjusting to life without a gallbladder. But with a bit of strategy, you can stock your kitchen with nutritious, digestible foods without breaking the bank.

First, embrace the power of planning. Before heading to the store, take some time to map out your meals for the week. This not only helps you stay on track with your dietary needs but also prevents impulse purchases that can quickly add up. Make a detailed shopping list based on your meal plan and stick to it—this way, you're buying only what you need.

Next, become a savvy shopper by taking advantage of sales and discounts. Keep an eye on weekly flyers and apps that highlight promotions. Buying in bulk, especially for staples like brown rice, quinoa, and canned beans, can save you money in the long run. These items have a long shelf life and are incredibly versatile, making them ideal for budget-friendly meal planning.

Don't overlook the power of store brands. Often, these products are just as good as their name-brand counterparts but come at a fraction of the cost. Items like canned tomatoes, frozen vegetables, and whole grains can often be found in the store's own brand line, offering substantial savings.

Fresh produce can be one of the more expensive parts of your grocery bill, but there are ways to manage this cost. Buying in-season fruits and vegetables can significantly reduce expenses. Seasonal produce is not only cheaper but also fresher and more flavorful. When out-of-season produce is needed, consider frozen options. They are typically picked and frozen at peak ripeness, preserving their nutritional value and flavor while often costing less than fresh.

Another tip is to incorporate more plant-based proteins into your diet. Lentils, chickpeas, and beans are not only budget-friendly but also packed with nutrients and easy to digest. They can be used in a variety of dishes, from soups and stews to salads and grain bowls, providing a cost-effective way to maintain a balanced diet.

Lastly, minimize food waste by storing your groceries properly. Invest in airtight containers to keep dry goods fresh, and learn the best ways to store fruits and vegetables to extend their shelf life. Using leftovers creatively can also help stretch your grocery budget further, transforming yesterday's dinner into today's lunch with minimal additional cost.

By following these budget-friendly shopping tips, you can maintain a healthy, balanced diet that supports your post-gallbladder lifestyle while keeping your finances in check. This thoughtful approach to grocery shopping ensures that you nourish your body without unnecessary stress on your wallet.

3.2 KITCHEN TOOLS AND GADGETS FOR EASY MEAL PREP

Imagine your kitchen as a well-equipped workshop, where the right tools and gadgets make meal preparation not just easier but also more enjoyable. For anyone adapting to a post-gallbladder diet, having efficient kitchen tools can transform how you approach cooking.

First, consider the magic of a good blender. This versatile tool can whip up smoothies, soups, and sauces in minutes, making it invaluable for preparing nutritious, digestible meals. Opt for one with multiple speed settings and a sturdy build to handle various ingredients with ease.

Next, a quality set of knives is essential. Sharp, reliable knives make chopping vegetables, slicing meats, and dicing fruits quicker and safer. A chef's knife, a paring knife, and a serrated knife should cover most of your culinary needs.

A steamer basket is another must-have. Steaming vegetables retains their nutrients and makes them easier to digest, aligning perfectly with your new dietary requirements. It's a simple, inexpensive tool that can elevate the nutritional value of your meals.

Lastly, a slow cooker can be a game-changer. With a slow cooker, you can prepare hearty, low-fat meals with minimal effort. Just toss in your ingredients in the morning, and by dinner time, you have a delicious, ready-to-eat meal. It's perfect for making soups, stews, and even some lean protein dishes.

These tools and gadgets not only save time but also encourage healthier cooking habits, making your journey towards a balanced diet more effortless and enjoyable. Embrace these essentials, and let your kitchen work for you, creating meals that are both nourishing and delightful.

Imagine stepping into your kitchen, a sanctuary where culinary magic happens, with the knowledge that the right appliances can make your post-gallbladder diet not only manageable but truly enjoyable. Let's talk about those must-have appliances that will become your best allies in preparing meals that are both delicious and easy on your digestive system.

First on the list is a high-quality blender. This isn't just any blender, but a powerful one that can handle everything from smoothies to pureed soups. Smoothies become a quick, nutrient-packed breakfast option, blending fruits, vegetables, and supplements into a drink that's gentle on your stomach. Pureed soups, on the other hand, provide a comforting, easily digestible meal for lunch or dinner.

Next, consider a slow cooker. This appliance is a game-changer for anyone looking to prepare meals that are both flavorful and low in fat. Slow cooking allows you to infuse dishes with rich flavors without relying on heavy oils or fats. Imagine coming home to a pot of perfectly tender vegetables and lean proteins, ready to nourish you without the fuss.

An air fryer is another must-have. It allows you to enjoy the texture and taste of fried foods with a fraction of the fat. Whether it's crisping up some vegetables or cooking lean cuts of meat, the air fryer uses hot air circulation to create that desirable crispy finish without compromising your dietary needs.

Equally important is a steamer. Steamed vegetables retain their nutrients and are easier to digest. A good steamer can help you prepare everything from fish to a variety of veggies, ensuring that your meals are both healthy and satisfying.

Don't forget the importance of a food processor. Chopping, slicing, and dicing become effortless, saving you time and effort. This appliance is perfect for preparing ingredients for a wide range of dishes, ensuring you have consistent textures and flavors in every bite.

Finally, a rice cooker can be incredibly useful. Not just for rice, these appliances can often cook other grains like quinoa or barley, providing you with a variety of complex carbohydrates that are gentle on your digestive system.

Investing in these appliances transforms your kitchen into a haven of health, making it easier to stick to your dietary guidelines and ensuring every meal is a delight. Your journey to a smooth recovery and a healthy lifestyle is paved with the right tools, and these appliances are just the beginning.

Picture yourself in the midst of a busy weekday, with the clock ticking faster than you'd like, and yet you still want to prepare a meal that's both nourishing and gentle on your digestive system. This is where time-saving gadgets become your kitchen heroes, turning what could be a stressful cooking experience into an effortless and enjoyable one.

Consider the multi-cooker, a modern marvel that combines the functions of a pressure cooker, slow cooker, rice cooker, and more. With a multi-cooker, you can whip up a variety of dishes, from tender stews to perfectly cooked grains, all in one pot. Imagine setting it up in the morning, and by dinner, you have a flavorful, easily digestible meal waiting for you. It's like having a sous-chef that never needs a break.

Another indispensable gadget is the immersion blender. This handy tool allows you to blend soups, sauces, and smoothies directly in the pot or glass, cutting down on cleanup time. Instead of transferring hot liquids to a traditional blender and risking spills, you simply blend in place. It's perfect for creating those creamy soups and nutrient-rich smoothies that are gentle on your system.

For those who love their vegetables but hate the prep work, a mandoliner slicer can be a game-changer. This gadget allows you to slice, julienne, and dice vegetables quickly and uniformly. Whether you're preparing a fresh salad or cooking up a stir-fry, a mandoliner makes the process fast and the results consistently beautiful.

In the realm of chopping and dicing, an electric chopper can save you countless minutes. These compact devices make quick work of onions, garlic, herbs, and more. Instead of spending precious time with a knife, you can have your ingredients ready in seconds, giving you more time to enjoy the cooking process and less time worrying about the prep.

And let's not forget the humble microwave, often underestimated but incredibly valuable for quick meal solutions. It's ideal for reheating leftovers, steaming vegetables, or even cooking whole meals when you're in a pinch. With the right approach, your microwave can help you prepare meals that are just as nutritious and satisfying as those cooked by conventional methods.

These gadgets don't just save time; they transform your cooking experience, making it easier to adhere to your post-gallbladder diet while managing a busy life. They bring efficiency and ease into your kitchen, allowing you to focus on what matters most—enjoying healthy, delicious meals without the stress.

Imagine walking into a kitchen where everything has its place, a haven of organization that makes cooking a breeze, especially when you're adapting to a new dietary regimen. Organizing your kitchen for efficiency is not just about tidiness; it's about creating a space that supports your culinary goals and makes meal preparation a joyful, stress-free experience.

Start by considering the layout of your kitchen. The key is to design your workspace around the concept of flow. Think about the tasks you perform most frequently and arrange your tools and ingredients accordingly. For instance, keep your chopping board, knives, and fresh produce close together. This way, when you start preparing a meal, you can move seamlessly from washing vegetables to chopping them without unnecessary steps.

One often overlooked but incredibly effective strategy is to keep your most-used items within arm's reach. Open shelves or easily accessible cabinets can store your everyday pots, pans, and utensils. Imagine reaching for your favorite skillet without having to dig through a cluttered cabinet. This simple adjustment can make a significant difference in your cooking efficiency.

Pantry organization is another critical aspect. Clear containers not only help keep your ingredients fresh but also allow you to see at a glance what's inside. Labeling these containers can save you time, especially when you're in a hurry. A well-organized pantry means you'll spend less time searching for ingredients and more time enjoying the cooking process.

Don't forget the importance of a designated prep area. A clean, clutter-free countertop provides the perfect space to prepare your meals. Keep this area free of non-essential items, reserving it exclusively for meal prep. It's a small change, but having a dedicated space can streamline your cooking and make it more enjoyable.

Lastly, consider the role of cleaning supplies in your kitchen's efficiency. Having a tidy, well-organized cleaning station means you can quickly clean as you go, preventing messes from piling up. This keeps your kitchen inviting and functional, ready for the next culinary adventure.

By creating an organized, efficient kitchen, you set the stage for culinary success. It transforms meal preparation from a chore into a pleasant, even meditative activity. With everything in its place, you can focus on what truly matters: crafting meals that nourish your body and soul.

Picture a serene Sunday afternoon, where the week ahead lies open and full of promise. This is the perfect time to dive into meal planning and grocery shopping, turning what can often feel like a chore into a pleasant ritual that sets you up for culinary success. Meal planning and efficient shopping are cornerstones of maintaining a diet that's both nutritious and easy on your digestive system.

Begin by envisioning your week's meals. Think about the flavors and ingredients that excite you, but also keep in mind the dietary adjustments needed post-surgery. A balanced approach is key. Start with a simple plan: jot down ideas for breakfast, lunch, and dinner, considering how leftovers might be creatively repurposed. This not only saves time but ensures variety in your diet.

A practical tip is to base your meals around versatile ingredients. For instance, a batch of quinoa can serve as a side for dinner, a base for a lunch salad, and an addition to a breakfast bowl. By planning meals that share common ingredients, you reduce waste and streamline your grocery list.

Speaking of grocery lists, make it your secret weapon. A well-thought-out list can transform your shopping experience, making it efficient and stress-free. Organize your list by sections of the grocery store—produce, dairy, grains, proteins—so you can easily navigate the aisles. This helps you stick to your plan and avoid impulse buys that might not align with your dietary needs.

Don't underestimate the power of seasonal produce. Not only is it often fresher and more flavorful, but it can also be more affordable. Plan your meals around what's in season, and you'll find yourself enjoying a variety of fruits and vegetables that enhance your dishes and your health.

Another smart strategy is to allocate some time for prep as soon as you return from shopping. Washing and chopping vegetables, marinating proteins, and portioning out snacks can save you valuable minutes during the week. This prep work turns meal times into a seamless process, where everything is ready to be cooked or assembled with minimal effort.

By approaching meal planning and grocery shopping with a sense of creativity and organization, you set the stage for a week of delicious, easy-to-digest meals. It's not just about the food; it's about creating a rhythm and routine that supports your health and well-being, allowing you to enjoy the process as much as the meals themselves.

Imagine a calm, reflective Saturday morning where you sit with a cup of herbal tea, the aroma filling your kitchen, and a blank planner in front of you. This is the perfect moment to craft a weekly meal plan, a tool that not only brings structure to your days but also ensures you stay on track with your dietary needs post-gallbladder surgery.

Start by considering the balance and variety you want in your diet. Each meal should be an opportunity to nourish your body, so think about incorporating a mix of lean proteins, whole grains, and an array of colorful vegetables. Aim for diversity in your meals to keep your palate interested and your body well-nourished.

Begin with breakfast. For many, this is the foundation of the day. Plan for quick, digestible options like smoothies, overnight oats, or scrambled egg whites with spinach. These meals should be easy to prepare yet packed with the nutrients you need to kickstart your day.

For lunch, consider meals that can double as leftovers from dinner. This not only saves time but also reduces food waste. For instance, a roasted chicken dinner can become a hearty salad the next day, or a vegetable stir-fry can turn into a filling wrap. Think about meals that are simple to prepare yet satisfying and gentle on your digestive system.

Dinner can be a time to unwind and enjoy a more elaborate meal. Plan for dishes that bring you comfort and are easy to digest. This could be anything from a soothing bowl of soup to a baked fish with steamed vegetables. The goal is to create meals that are both delicious and beneficial for your health.

Snacks and small bites are just as important. Keep them in mind as you plan, choosing options that are easy to prepare and carry with you. Fresh fruits, nuts, and yogurt can make for great mid-morning or afternoon snacks, ensuring you stay energized throughout the day.

Don't forget to leave room for flexibility. Life can be unpredictable, and your meal plan should accommodate that. Maybe designate one night a week for a "flex meal" where you can try something new or use up leftovers creatively. This keeps the process enjoyable and less rigid.

By thoughtfully creating a weekly meal plan, you set yourself up for success. It's not just about the food on your plate, but about crafting a lifestyle that supports your health, well-being, and joy in eating. This approach transforms meal times into moments of nourishment and satisfaction, making your journey post-surgery a smooth and flavorful adventure.

Imagine the hustle and bustle of a grocery store, aisles lined with endless options, and a cart in your hands ready to be filled with nutritious choices. Efficient grocery shopping is not just about speed; it's about strategy and mindfulness, ensuring that you leave the store with everything you need to support your healthy, post-gallbladder diet.

Before you even set foot in the store, preparation is key. Start by crafting a detailed shopping list based on your weekly meal plan. This list is your roadmap, guiding you through the aisles and helping you stay focused. Group items by category—produce, dairy, grains—so you can quickly locate what you need without backtracking.

Timing your shopping trips can also make a huge difference. Try to go during off-peak hours, such as early mornings or late evenings. This not only makes for a more pleasant shopping experience but also allows you to navigate the store more efficiently without the crowds. Imagine leisurely walking through a serene, well-stocked store, easily finding everything on your list.

As you move through the store, stick to the perimeter where the fresh foods are typically located. Fresh fruits and vegetables, lean proteins, and dairy products are often found here. The center aisles usually contain processed and packaged foods that might not align with your dietary goals. By focusing on the perimeter, you fill your cart with wholesome, nutritious ingredients.

When choosing produce, opt for seasonal fruits and vegetables. They are not only fresher and more flavorful but often more affordable. Take a moment to admire the vibrant colors and imagine the delicious, digestible meals you will create. Shopping seasonally also introduces variety into your diet, keeping your meals interesting and balanced.

Be mindful of labels and ingredients, especially when selecting packaged items. Look for products with minimal ingredients and avoid those with added sugars and unhealthy fats. Reading labels becomes second nature, empowering you to make informed choices that support your health.

Consider bulk-buying staples that you use frequently, such as grains, nuts, and spices. This not only saves money but also ensures you always have essential ingredients on hand. Picture your pantry, neatly stocked with jars of quinoa, almonds, and fragrant herbs, ready to be transformed into delicious meals.

Finally, don't forget the importance of reusable bags. They are an eco-friendly choice and often sturdier than plastic, making it easier to carry your groceries home. Plus, there's something satisfying about unpacking your fresh finds from a bag that reflects your commitment to a healthier lifestyle and a healthier planet.

Efficient grocery shopping is about creating a system that works for you, turning what could be a mundane task into an enjoyable, purposeful activity. With a little planning and mindfulness, you can navigate the grocery store with ease, filling your cart with ingredients that will nourish your body and delight your senses.

Imagine opening your refrigerator to find it not just filled with fresh, vibrant ingredients, but also remarkably organized, with nothing going to waste. Reducing food waste is not just a matter of saving money; it's a practice that benefits your health, the environment, and the overall enjoyment of your culinary experiences.

Start by planning your meals with intention. When you create your weekly meal plan, think about how ingredients can be used across multiple dishes. For instance, if you're buying a bunch of carrots, plan to use them in a stir-fry, as a snack with hummus, and in a hearty soup. This way, you maximize the utility of each ingredient and ensure nothing is forgotten in the back of the fridge.

Storage techniques play a crucial role in reducing waste. Properly storing fruits and vegetables can significantly extend their life. Leafy greens, for instance, stay fresher when wrapped in a damp cloth and placed in a sealed container. Herbs can be stored upright in a glass of water, much like flowers, to keep them vibrant longer. Imagine the satisfaction of reaching for a sprig of parsley that's as fresh as the day you bought it.

Embrace the art of leftovers. Transforming last night's dinner into today's lunch is not only efficient but can lead to some surprisingly delicious creations. Think of a roasted chicken dinner that turns into a flavorful chicken salad or a vegetable medley that becomes the star of a frittata. By viewing leftovers as an opportunity rather than an inconvenience, you cultivate a kitchen culture that values every bite.

Another effective strategy is to conduct regular inventory checks. Before heading to the grocery store, take a moment to scan your pantry and fridge. This helps you avoid buying duplicates and encourages you to use up what you already have. Picture a well-organized kitchen where every item has a purpose and a place, making meal preparation a breeze.

Composting is a fantastic way to deal with unavoidable waste like vegetable peels and coffee grounds. Even if you don't have a garden, many communities offer composting programs. By composting, you return valuable nutrients to the soil and reduce the amount of waste that ends up in landfills.

CHAPTER 4: BREAKFASTS FOR A GENTLE START

4.1 QUICK AND EASY LOW-FAT BREAKFASTS

Imagine waking up each morning to a breakfast that's not only light on the stomach but also inviting and flavorful. For many who have undergone gallbladder surgery, the morning meal can often seem like a challenge. However, embracing a low-fat diet doesn't mean sacrificing enjoyment—especially when you know exactly how to start your day with the right kind of foods.

Quick and easy low-fat breakfasts are a cornerstone for a smooth recovery and maintaining digestive health post-surgery. The key here is to integrate ingredients that are easy to digest, support your healing, and still tickle your taste buds. So, let's walk through some ideas that embody comfort, health, and simplicity, without the worry of complicated preparations.

The Simple Pleasure of Overnight Oats

Consider overnight oats—a splendid option that waits to greet you first thing in the morning. The beauty of this dish is in its simplicity and versatility. Start with plain rolled oats—which are an excellent source of soluble fiber and can aid in gentle digestion. Mix these oats with your choice of a low-fat milk alternative—perhaps almond or coconut milk, which are lighter on the stomach yet creamy enough to give that comforting texture.

To sweeten, steer clear of refined sugars; opt instead for a dash of natural sweetness from honey or a sprinkle of dried fruits. Add a few slices of banana or a handful of berries for their soothing qualities and antioxidants. Prepared the night before, this dish enhances in flavor overnight and requires no morning prep time—perfect for easing into your day without stress.

Light and Satisfying Egg White Omelets

Egg whites are an excellent source of protein that's low in fat and easy on the stomach. Creating an omelet with egg whites, fresh spinach, and a touch of herbs can offer a delightful and nutritious start to the day. Spinach is not only low in fat but also packed with fiber and important nutrients like magnesium, which aids the digestive system. Throw in some chopped bell peppers for a nice crunch and a boost of vitamin C.

Cooking these ingredients in a non-stick skillet with just a drizzle of olive oil ensures your meal remains as low-fat as possible. Using herbs such as dill or parsley can elevate the flavor without needing much salt, which is beneficial for maintaining a healthy water balance in the body.

Muffins and Breads—with a Twist

The aroma of freshly baked muffins or bread can be very inviting in the morning. By modifying traditional recipes to fit a low-fat diet, you can enjoy this pleasure without any guilt. Use whole grain flours to provide the necessary fiber and nutrients. Applesauce makes an excellent substitute for oil or butter in these recipes, adding natural sweetness and moisture without the fat.

Incorporate blueberries or raspberries for their antioxidants, or throw in a handful of nuts for their omega-3 fatty acids, which are essential for inflammation reduction and overall health. Baking a batch during the weekend can serve as a quick breakfast option throughout the week—just reheat briefly in the microwave for a warm, satisfying start to your day.

Embracing Yogurt's Versatility

Low-fat yogurt is another staple for a nourishing, post-gallbladder removal diet. It's soft and easy to digest, plus rich in probiotics, which are beneficial for gut health. Blend yogurt with granola and a drizzle of honey, or layer it with fruits to make a scrumptious parfait. The probiotics in yogurt help in maintaining a healthy balance of gut bacteria, which is crucial after your digestive system has undergone changes post-surgery.

Alternatively, consider adding a swirl of almond butter for a protein boost or sprinkle in some chia seeds for their fiber content. The natural tang of the yogurt pairs wonderfully with the sweetness of the fruit and the richness of the nuts, creating a deeply satisfying yet light breakfast.

Through these breakfast options, what unfolds is a narrative that marries convenience with health and taste. Navigating a low-fat diet in the early hours doesn't have to be complicated or bland. Each of these meals is designed to ensure that you start your day not just by feeding your body what it needs to recover and thrive without a gallbladder but also by pleasing your palate. The warmth of a lightly spiced muffin, the freshness of a fruit-layered parfait, the comforting simplicity of soft oats, and the nourishing freshness of an egg white omelet—each dish brings its own story of recovery, health, and delight.

As you adapt to this new dietary routine, remember that your breakfast sets the tone for the day. A gentle, low-fat start not only supports your digestive health but also uplifts your spirit, reassuring you that yes, diet restrictions can indeed come with their own joy and flavor. This is more than just about eating right; it's about embracing a lifestyle that accommodates change positively and deliciously. Here's to many beautiful mornings filled with good health and great taste!

BERRY OVERNIGHT OATS

PREPARATION TIME: 5 min - **COOKING TIME:** None

MODE OF COOKING: Refrigeration - **SERVINGS:** 2

INGREDIENTS:
- 1 cup rolled oats
- 1 cup unsweetened almond milk
- 1/2 cup low-fat Greek yogurt
- 1/2 cup mixed berries (strawberries, blueberries, raspberries)
- 1 Tbsp chia seeds
- 1 tsp honey (optional)

PROCEDURE:
1. In a medium-sized bowl, combine the oats, almond milk, Greek yogurt, mixed berries, and chia seeds.
2. Stir well to mix all ingredients thoroughly.
3. Cover the bowl and refrigerate overnight.
4. In the morning, give it a good stir, add honey if desired, and serve.

TIPS:
1. Use frozen berries if fresh ones are not available.
2. Add a splash of vanilla extract for extra flavor.
3. Top with a few extra berries and a sprinkle of nuts before serving.

NUTRITIONAL VALUES:
Calories: 210, Fat: 3g, Carbs: 37g, Protein: 10g, Sugar: 9g, Cholesterol: 5mg, Fiber: 7g

VANILLA MAPLE YOGURT PARFAIT

PREPARATION TIME: 10 min - **COOKING TIME:** None

MODE OF COOKING: None - **SERVINGS:** 2

INGREDIENTS:
- 1 cup low-fat Greek yogurt
- 1/4 cup granola (low-fat, low-sugar)
- 1/4 cup fresh blueberries
- 1/4 cup fresh strawberries, sliced
- 1 Tbsp pure maple syrup
- 1/2 tsp vanilla extract

PROCEDURE:
1. In a small bowl, mix the Greek yogurt, maple syrup, and vanilla extract until well combined.
2. In two serving glasses, layer the yogurt mixture, granola, and berries. Start with a layer of yogurt, then granola, and then berries. Repeat the layers.
3. Finish with a few berries on top for garnish.
4. Serve immediately for a crunchy parfait or let it sit for a few minutes if you prefer the granola to soften slightly.

TIPS:
1. Substitute granola with crushed nuts or seeds for a different texture.
2. Use any seasonal fruits available to vary the flavors.
3. Add a pinch of cinnamon to the yogurt mixture for a warm flavor note.

NUTRITIONAL VALUES:
Calories: 180, Fat: 2g, Carbs: 29g, Protein: 11g, Sugar: 15g, Cholesterol: 5mg, Fiber: 4g

BANANA OAT MUFFINS

PREPARATION TIME: 10 min - **COOKING TIME:** 20 min

MODE OF COOKING: Baking - **SERVINGS:** 12 muffins

INGREDIENTS:
- 2 ripe bananas, mashed
- 1 cup rolled oats
- 1/2 cup low-fat Greek yogurt
- 1/4 cup honey
- 1 tsp baking powder
- 1/2 tsp baking soda

PROCEDURE:

1. Preheat oven to 350°F (175°C) and line a muffin tin with paper liners.

2. In a large bowl, combine mashed bananas, oats, Greek yogurt, and honey. Mix well.

3. Add baking powder and baking soda to the mixture, stirring until fully combined.

4. Spoon the batter into the muffin tin, filling each cup about 3/4 full.

5. Bake for 20 minutes or until a toothpick inserted into the center comes out clean.

6. Allow muffins to cool in the tin for a few minutes before transferring to a wire rack to cool completely.

TIPS:

1. Add a handful of raisins or nuts for extra texture and flavor.

2. Store in an airtight container for up to three days.

3. Freeze any extras for a quick breakfast option later.

NUTRITIONAL VALUES: Calories: 110, Fat: 1g, Carbs: 23g, Protein: 3g, Sugar: 8g, Cholesterol: 0mg, Fiber: 2g

---

APPLE CINNAMON BREAD

PREPARATION TIME: 15 min - **COOKING TIME:** 45 min

MODE OF COOKING: Baking - **SERVINGS:** 8 slices

INGREDIENTS:

- 1 1/2 cups whole wheat flour
- 1/2 cup unsweetened applesauce
- 1/2 cup almond milk
- 1/4 cup honey
- 1 tsp baking powder
- 1 tsp cinnamon
- 1 apple, peeled and finely chopped

PROCEDURE:

1. Preheat oven to 350°F (175°C) and grease a loaf pan.

2. In a large bowl, combine whole wheat flour, baking powder, and cinnamon.

3. In another bowl, mix applesauce, almond milk, and honey.

4. Pour the wet ingredients into the dry ingredients and stir until just combined.

5. Fold in the chopped apple.

6. Pour the batter into the prepared loaf pan and smooth the top.

7. Bake for 45 minutes or until a toothpick inserted into the center comes out clean.

8. Let the bread cool in the pan for 10 minutes, then transfer to a wire rack to cool completely.

TIPS:

1. Sprinkle a bit of extra cinnamon on top before baking for added flavor.

2. Use a variety of apples for a more complex taste.

3. Serve with a thin spread of low-fat cream cheese for a delicious treat.

NUTRITIONAL VALUES:

Calories: 140, Fat: 1.5g, Carbs: 30g, Protein: 3g, Sugar: 10g, Cholesterol: 0mg, Fiber: 4g

---

SPINACH AND MUSHROOM EGG WHITE OMELET

PREPARATION TIME: 5 min - **COOKING TIME:** 10 min

MODE OF COOKING: Stovetop - **SERVINGS:** 1

INGREDIENTS:

- 4 egg whites
- 1/2 cup fresh spinach, chopped
- 1/4 cup mushrooms, sliced
- 1 Tbsp low-fat milk
- 1 tsp olive oil
- Salt and pepper to taste

PROCEDURE:

1. In a bowl, whisk the egg whites with the low-fat milk until frothy. Season with salt and pepper.

2. Heat the olive oil in a non-stick skillet over medium heat.

3. Add the mushrooms and sauté for 2-3 minutes until they soften.

4. Add the chopped spinach and cook for another minute until wilted.

5. Pour the egg white mixture over the vegetables in the skillet.

6. Cook for 3-4 minutes, lifting the edges with a spatula to let the uncooked egg flow underneath.

7. Once the eggs are set, fold the omelet in half and slide it onto a plate. Serve immediately.

TIPS:

1. Add a sprinkle of low-fat cheese for extra flavor.

2. Serve with a side of whole-grain toast for a more substantial breakfast.

3. Use any leftover vegetables you have on hand to vary the omelet.

NUTRITIONAL VALUES:
Calories: 120, Fat: 3g, Carbs: 4g, Protein: 18g, Sugar: 2g, Cholesterol: 0mg, Fiber: 1g

TOMATO AND BASIL EGG WHITE OMELET

PREPARATION TIME: 5 min - **COOKING TIME:** 10 min
MODE OF COOKING: Stovetop - **SERVINGS:** 1
INGREDIENTS:
- 4 egg whites
- 1 small tomato, diced
- 2 Tbsp fresh basil, chopped
- 1 Tbsp low-fat milk
- 1 tsp olive oil
- Salt and pepper to taste

PROCEDURE:
1. In a bowl, whisk the egg whites with the low-fat milk until frothy. Season with salt and pepper.

2. Heat the olive oil in a non-stick skillet over medium heat.

3. Add the diced tomato and cook for 2 minutes until it begins to soften.

4. Pour the egg white mixture over the tomato in the skillet.

5. Cook for 3-4 minutes, lifting the edges with a spatula to let the uncooked egg flow underneath.

6. Sprinkle the chopped basil over the omelet.

7. Once the eggs are set, fold the omelet in half and slide it onto a plate. Serve immediately.

TIPS:
1. Add a pinch of garlic powder for extra flavor.

2. Serve with a side of mixed greens for a light and nutritious meal.

3. Substitute basil with fresh parsley or cilantro for a different taste.

NUTRITIONAL VALUES:
Calories: 115, Fat: 3g, Carbs: 5g, Protein: 17g, Sugar: 3g, Cholesterol: 0mg, Fiber: 1g

4.2 HIGH-FIBER BREAKFAST OPTIONS

Starting your day without a gallbladder can be challenging, but choosing the right breakfast can set a positive tone for your digestive system and overall well-being. High-fiber options are particularly beneficial as they contribute to smoother digestion and provide a sustained release of energy, crucial for those adjusting to a new dietary lifestyle post-surgery.

Imagine waking up to a morning where breakfast isn't just a meal but a nurturing start that supports your digestive health. For many of us who have undergone gallbladder surgery, the thought of breakfast brings about a cloud of uncertainty—what to eat that's both satisfying and gentle on the digestive system? Let's delve into the world of high-fiber breakfasts, which offer not just comfort but also a promise of well-being.

Fiber is a cornerstone in the diet of individuals without a gallbladder. It helps in the gradual absorption of nutrients, which is crucial because your bile—a digestive fluid that was once regulated by your gallbladder—is now flowing more continuously into your intestines. A high-fiber breakfast aids in controlling the flow of bile, which can help prevent discomfort and problems like bile acid diarrhea.

Whole grain cereals, for instance, are a fantastic choice to commence your day. Opting for grains like oats, barley, or quinoa not only provides the necessary fiber but also packs essential nutrients such as B vitamins, iron, and magnesium. These grains become particularly comforting when served warm, mingled with a hint of cinnamon and perhaps a splash of almond milk, which is gentle on the stomach and low in fat.

Moving on to smoothies, which are a splendid way to ingest a concentrated dose of fiber and nutrients without stressing the digestive system. A fiber-rich smoothie might include ingredients like spinach or kale, coupled with a high-fiber fruit such as raspberries or blueberries. Add a spoonful of chia seeds to elevate the fiber content and create a texture that is not only pleasing to the palate but also beneficial for digestion. The smooth magic of blending these components together results in a drink that's both refreshing and filling—a perfect conciliant for the mornings when you need a quick, nutritious solution.

Another excellent choice for a high-fiber morning meal is a breakfast bowl loaded with various textures and flavors. Start with a base of Greek yogurt to add a protein punch without excess fat. Top it with a generous helping of mixed berries, nuts, and perhaps a sprinkle of flaxseed for an additional fiber boost. Each spoonful is a marriage of creaminess from the yogurt and a satisfying crunch from the nuts, making each bite a delightful experience for the senses.

But why is all this focus on fiber beneficial specifically for those without a gallbladder? Beyond aiding digestion, fiber helps in regulating blood sugar levels, providing a steady supply of energy throughout the morning and preventing midday crashes. This is particularly important because maintaining stable energy levels can be a challenge in the recovery phase post-surgery.

Moreover, adopting a high-fiber diet can also have long-term health benefits, including reduced risks of heart disease and better weight management—factors that are crucial considering the digestive adjustments your body is making in the absence of a gallbladder by incorporating more fiber into your breakfast, you lay a strong foundation for not just the day, but a healthier lifestyle.

As we talk about adjustments, it's important to address the variety and how one can rotate through these options to bring joy and anticipation to morning meals. After all, variety is not just the spice of life but also a key to maintaining a nutritious diet that keeps you deeply connected to your food and body's needs.

Lastly, embracing a refreshing approach to breakfast not only deploys well-being but also empowers one with the sense that through mindful eating, we can handle our health post-surgery with confidence. Each high-fiber bite is a step towards reconciling with one's body and its new way of digesting, absorbing, and thriving.

CREAMY BUCKWHEAT PORRIDGE

PREPARATION TIME: 5 min - **COOKING TIME:** 15 min

MODE OF COOKING: Stovetop - **SERVINGS:** 2

INGREDIENTS:

- 1/2 cup buckwheat groats
- 1 cup water
- 1 cup low-fat milk
- 1 Tbsp honey
- 1/2 tsp cinnamon
- 1/4 cup fresh blueberries
-

PROCEDURE:

1. In a medium pot, bring the buckwheat groats and water to a boil.

2. Reduce heat, cover, and simmer for 10 minutes until water is absorbed.

3. Stir in the low-fat milk, honey, and cinnamon. Cook for an additional 5 minutes until creamy.

4. Divide into bowls and top with fresh blueberries. Serve warm.

TIPS:

1. Substitute honey with maple syrup or agave nectar for a different sweetness.

2. Add a handful of nuts for extra crunch and protein.

3. Use almond or oat milk for a dairy-free version.

NUTRITIONAL VALUES:

Calories: 220, Fat: 2g, Carbs: 44g, Protein: 8g, Sugar: 12g, Cholesterol: 5mg, Fiber: 6g

SPICED AMARANTH CEREAL

PREPARATION TIME: 5 min - **COOKING TIME:** 20 min

MODE OF COOKING: Stovetop - **SERVINGS:** 2

INGREDIENTS:

- 1/2 cup amaranth
- 1 1/2 cups water
- 1/2 cup low-fat milk
- 1 Tbsp maple syrup
- 1/2 tsp ground ginger
- 1/4 tsp ground cloves
- 1/4 cup diced apple

PROCEDURE:

1. In a saucepan, combine amaranth and water. Bring to a boil.

2. Reduce heat to low, cover, and simmer for 15 minutes until water is absorbed.

3. Stir in low-fat milk, maple syrup, ground ginger, and ground cloves. Cook for another 5 minutes, stirring frequently.

4. Divide into bowls and top with diced apple. Serve warm.

TIPS:

1. Add a sprinkle of nutmeg for an extra layer of flavor.

2. Use pear or banana instead of apple for variety.

3. Prepare a larger batch and store in the refrigerator for a quick breakfast option during the week.

NUTRITIONAL VALUES:

Calories: 240, Fat: 3g, Carbs: 47g, Protein: 9g, Sugar: 10g, Cholesterol: 5mg, Fiber: 7g

BERRY FLAXSEED SMOOTHIE

PREPARATION TIME: 5 min - **COOKING TIME:** None

MODE OF COOKING: Blending - **SERVINGS:** 2

INGREDIENTS:

- 1 cup mixed berries (strawberries, blueberries, raspberries)
- 1 banana
- 1 cup unsweetened almond milk
- 2 Tbsp ground flaxseed
- 1 Tbsp honey (optional)
- 1/2 cup ice cubes

PROCEDURE:

1. Combine mixed berries, banana, almond milk, ground flaxseed, honey, and ice cubes in a blender.

2. Blend until smooth and creamy.

3. Pour into glasses and serve immediately.

TIPS:

1. Use frozen berries to make the smoothie extra cold and thick.

2. Add a handful of spinach for an extra nutrient boost.

3. Adjust the sweetness by varying the amount of honey or omitting it altogether.

NUTRITIONAL VALUES:

Calories: 180, Fat: 5g, Carbs: 36g, Protein: 4g, Sugar: 20g, Cholesterol: 0mg, Fiber: 8g

GREEN CHIA SEED SMOOTHIE

PREPARATION TIME: 5 min - **COOKING TIME:** None

MODE OF COOKING: Blending - **SERVINGS:** 2

INGREDIENTS:

- 1 cup spinach
- 1/2 avocado
- 1 apple, cored and chopped
- 1 cup coconut water
- 2 Tbsp chia seeds
- 1/2 cup ice cubes

PROCEDURE:

1. Combine spinach, avocado, apple, coconut water, chia seeds, and ice cubes in a blender.

2. Blend until smooth and well combined.

3. Pour into glasses and serve immediately.

TIPS:

1. Use kale instead of spinach for a different green flavor.

2. Add a squeeze of lime juice for a tangy twist.

3. Let the chia seeds soak in the coconut water for 5 minutes before blending for a thicker texture.

NUTRITIONAL VALUES:

Calories: 160, Fat: 9g, Carbs: 20g, Protein: 3g, Sugar: 10g, Cholesterol: 0mg, Fiber: 8g

TROPICAL QUINOA BREAKFAST BOWL

PREPARATION TIME: 10 min - **COOKING TIME:** 15 min

MODE OF COOKING: Stovetop - **SERVINGS:** 2

INGREDIENTS:

- 1/2 cup quinoa, rinsed
- 1 cup water
- 1/2 cup unsweetened coconut milk
- 1 banana, sliced
- 1/2 cup diced pineapple
- 2 Tbsp shredded coconut
- 2 Tbsp chopped almonds

PROCEDURE:

1. In a pot, combine quinoa and water. Bring to a boil, reduce heat, cover, and simmer for 12-15 minutes until water is absorbed.

2. Stir in coconut milk and cook for an additional 2-3 minutes until creamy.

3. Divide quinoa into bowls, top with banana slices, pineapple, shredded coconut, and chopped almonds. Serve warm.

TIPS:

1. Use mango instead of pineapple for a different tropical flavor.

2. Add a drizzle of honey for extra sweetness.

3. Prepare quinoa ahead of time and refrigerate for quick assembly in the morning.

NUTRITIONAL VALUES:

Calories: 320, Fat: 10g, Carbs: 54g, Protein: 6g, Sugar: 18g, Cholesterol: 0mg, Fiber: 7g

APPLE CINNAMON CHIA PUDDING BOWL

PREPARATION TIME: 5 min - **COOKING TIME:** None (overnight)

MODE OF COOKING: Refrigeration - **SERVINGS:** 2

INGREDIENTS:

- 1/4 cup chia seeds
- 1 cup unsweetened almond milk
- 1 apple, diced
- 1 tsp cinnamon
- 1 Tbsp maple syrup
- 2 Tbsp chopped walnuts

PROCEDURE:

1. In a bowl, mix chia seeds, almond milk, and maple syrup. Stir well.

2. Cover and refrigerate overnight.

3. In the morning, stir the chia pudding and divide into bowls.

4. Top with diced apple, cinnamon, and chopped walnuts. Serve immediately.

TIPS:

1. Use pears instead of apples for a seasonal variation.

2. Add a sprinkle of nutmeg for extra warmth.

3. Store leftover chia pudding in an airtight container for up to three days.

NUTRITIONAL VALUES:

Calories: 220, Fat: 10g, Carbs: 30g, Protein: 5g, Sugar: 14g, Cholesterol: 0mg, Fiber: 11g

A day starts a bit brighter when you welcome it with a nourishing blend of flavors that not only satisfies your taste buds but also comforts your digestive system, especially when you're navigating life without a gallbladder. The journey of embracing a post-gallbladder removal diet can seem daunting, yet with the right tools—like refreshing and easy-to-digest smoothies and shakes—you can get your day off to an energizing and gentle start.

When we talk about smoothies and shakes, it's not just about throwing a bunch of ingredients in a blender. We're sculpting a morning ritual that integrates seamlessly into your new dietary lifestyle, offering a nutritional boost without overwhelming your digestive tract. The key here is to focus on ingredients that are inherently supportive of digestive health and understanding how these can replace more traditional, richer breakfast options that might not agree with your system anymore.

After the removal of the gallbladder, your body continues to produce bile, but it lacks the storage reservoir to release it effectively when consuming fatty meals. Therefore, smoothies and shakes present a brilliant solution. They can be tailored to be low in fat, yet high in essential nutrients, which aids digestion and ensures that you're not stressing your system early in the morning.

Green Smoothies: Including a variety of leafy greens such as spinach, kale, or Swiss chard is a wonderful strategy. Leafy greens are not only packed with essential nutrients and fiber but also have a high-water content, which helps to hydrate and soothe the digestive system. Imagine starting your day not just with a meal but with a glass of vitality—one that builds you up without setting you back in your recovery.

Protein-Packed Shakes: Post-surgery, your body needs adequate protein to heal and maintain muscle strength. Incorporating plant-based proteins such as pea protein, hemp seeds, or silken tofu into your shakes can provide the necessary protein without the high fat content that animal products often contribute. These ingredients blend beautifully into a creamy, satisfying shake that supports tissue repair and muscle health without overburdening your digestion.

But it's not just about the physical nourishment—flavor is equally crucial. Integrating fresh or frozen berries, which are low in fat and high in antioxidants, can enhance the taste and up the health quotient of your smoothie or shake. Berries like blueberries, raspberries, and strawberries bring a delightful freshness and are kind to your gut, acting as a natural sweetener and flavor enhancer.

Moreover, spices and herbs such as ginger, turmeric, and mint not only add a burst of flavor but also come with impressive anti-inflammatory properties and digestion-aiding potential. A smoothie infused with ginger can alleviate nausea and soothe the stomach, while mint can help reduce bloating and aid in smoother digestion.

Then there are the culinary techniques which can make this transition a creative and enjoyable process. For instance, when we think about the texture, which plays a crucial role in how enjoyable these drinks are, using a high-powered blender can achieve a silky-smooth texture that makes even the simplest ingredients feel luxurious. This is essential, as post-surgery, rough or grainy textures might be less tolerated, and a smooth, well-blended shake can be more comforting to the stomach. Personalization is also key in adapting to your new dietary needs. Trial and error have a place in your kitchen now more than ever. It's about finding what ingredients help you feel your best. Perhaps a combination of almond milk, banana, a spoonful of almond butter, and a dash of cinnamon causes no discomfort and becomes your go-to morning shake. Or, maybe you find that adding a scoop of avocado to your berry smoothie adds the creamy texture you've missed, without the digestive stress.

SPINACH AND AVOCADO GREEN SMOOTHIE

PREPARATION TIME: 5 min - **COOKING TIME:** None

MODE OF COOKING: Blending - **SERVINGS:** 2

INGREDIENTS:
- 1 cup fresh spinach
- 1/2 avocado
- 1 banana
- 1 cup unsweetened almond milk
- 1 Tbsp chia seeds
- 1/2 cup ice cubes

PROCEDURE:
1. Combine spinach, avocado, banana, almond milk, chia seeds, and ice cubes in a blender.
2. Blend until smooth and creamy.
3. Pour into glasses and serve immediately.

TIPS:
1. Add a squeeze of lemon juice for extra freshness.
2. Use frozen banana slices for a thicker texture.
3. Garnish with a few chia seeds on top for added crunch.

NUTRITIONAL VALUES:
Calories: 180, Fat: 9g, Carbs: 24g, Protein: 4g, Sugar: 10g, Cholesterol: 0mg, Fiber: 8g

KALE AND PINEAPPLE GREEN SMOOTHIE

PREPARATION TIME: 5 min - **COOKING TIME:** None

MODE OF COOKING: Blending - **SERVINGS:** 2

INGREDIENTS:
- 1 cup kale leaves, stems removed
- 1/2 cup fresh pineapple chunks
- 1/2 cucumber, peeled and chopped
- 1 cup coconut water
- 1 Tbsp ground flaxseed
- 1/2 cup ice cubes

PROCEDURE:
1. Combine kale, pineapple, cucumber, coconut water, ground flaxseed, and ice cubes in a blender.
2. Blend until smooth and well combined.
3. Pour into glasses and serve immediately.

TIPS:
1. Add a few mint leaves for a refreshing twist.
2. Use frozen pineapple for a chilled smoothie.
3. Adjust the thickness by adding more or less coconut water.

NUTRITIONAL VALUES:
Calories: 150, Fat: 3g, Carbs: 28g, Protein: 3g, Sugar: 14g, Cholesterol: 0mg, Fiber: 6g

CHOCOLATE BANANA PROTEIN SHAKE

PREPARATION TIME: 5 min - **COOKING TIME:** None

MODE OF COOKING: Blending - **SERVINGS:** 2

INGREDIENTS:
- 1 banana
- 1 cup unsweetened almond milk
- 1 scoop chocolate protein powder
- 1 Tbsp almond butter
- 1 Tbsp cocoa powder
- 1/2 cup ice cubes

PROCEDURE:
1. Combine banana, almond milk, chocolate protein powder, almond butter, cocoa powder, and ice cubes in a blender.
2. Blend until smooth and creamy.
3. Pour into glasses and serve immediately.

TIPS:
1. Use a frozen banana for a thicker texture.
2. Add a dash of cinnamon for extra flavor.
3. Adjust sweetness by adding a touch of honey if desired.

NUTRITIONAL VALUES:
Calories: 250, Fat: 8g, Carbs: 27g, Protein: 20g, Sugar: 12g, Cholesterol: 0mg, Fiber: 5g

BERRY VANILLA PROTEIN SHAKE

PREPARATION TIME: 5 min - **COOKING TIME:** None

MODE OF COOKING: Blending - **SERVINGS:** 2

INGREDIENTS:
- 1 cup mixed berries (strawberries, blueberries, raspberries)
- 1 cup unsweetened almond milk
- 1 scoop vanilla protein powder
- 1 Tbsp chia seeds

- 1/2 cup ice cubes

PROCEDURE:

1. Combine mixed berries, almond milk, vanilla protein powder, chia seeds, and ice cubes in a blender.

2. Blend until smooth and well combined.

3. Pour into glasses and serve immediately.

TIPS:

1. Use frozen berries for a colder, thicker shake.

2. Add a handful of spinach for an extra nutrient boost without altering the flavor.

3. Adjust the consistency by adding more almond milk if needed.

NUTRITIONAL VALUES:

Calories: 220, Fat: 5g, Carbs: 28g, Protein: 18g, Sugar: 15g, Cholesterol: 0mg, Fiber: 8g

---

TURMERIC GINGER IMMUNITY ELIXIR

PREPARATION TIME: 5 min - **COOKING TIME:** 10 min

MODE OF COOKING: Blending - **SERVINGS:** 2

INGREDIENTS:

- 1 cup coconut water
- 1/2-inch fresh ginger root, peeled
- 1/2 tsp turmeric powder
- 1/2 lemon, juiced
- 1 Tbsp honey

DIRECTIONS:

1. Combine all ingredients in a blender.
2. Blend until smooth.
3. Pour into glasses and serve immediately.

TIPS:

1. Add a pinch of black pepper to enhance turmeric absorption.
2. Use fresh turmeric root for a stronger flavor.

N.V.:

Calories: 45, Fat: 0.2g, Carbs: 12g, Protein: 0.5g, Sugar: 10g, Cholesterol: 0mg

---

PINEAPPLE MINT DIGESTIVE SMOOTHIE

PREPARATION TIME: 5 min - **COOKING TIME:** 5 min

MODE OF COOKING: Blending - **SERVINGS:** 2

INGREDIENTS:

- 1 cup fresh pineapple chunks
- 1/2 cup coconut milk
- 1/2 cup ice
- 1 Tbsp fresh mint leaves
- 1/2 tsp chia seeds

DIRECTIONS:

1. Combine all ingredients in a blender.

2. Blend until smooth.
3. Pour into glasses and serve immediately.

TIPS:

1. Freeze pineapple chunks for a thicker smoothie.
2. Garnish with extra mint leaves for added freshness.

N.V.:

Calories: 80, Fat: 4g, Carbs: 11g, Protein: 1g, Sugar: 9g, Cholesterol: 0mg

CHAPTER 5: LIGHT AND NOURISHING LUNCHES

5.1 LOW-FAT SOUPS AND STEWS

When embarking on a journey of recovery after gallbladder surgery, one of the primary adjustments any individual must make involves rethinking their approach to everyday meals. A crucial element to consider during this transition is the incorporation of low-fat soups and stews, which can be both comforting and nourishing. These dishes not only offer the softer, easy-to-digest qualities needed during the recovery phase but also provide versatility and depth in flavor that cater to both individual tastes and nutritional needs.

Imagine it is a cool evening, a scenario ideally suited for a warm bowl of soup. The steam rises, carrying with it the delicate aroma of simmering herbs and vegetables. For anyone adapting to life without a gallbladder, this isn't just dinner; it's a therapeutic embrace for the digestive system. A carefully crafted low-fat soup can deliver nutrients without the burden of high fat content that the body now struggles to process.

Starting with simple vegetable broths enriched with fresh herbs provides a foundation from which numerous variations can be built. The broth, whether made from scratch from chicken bones or vegetables, forms a nutrient-rich base that soothes the stomach and prepares the digestive system for more substantial foods. Adding lean proteins, such as shredded chicken breast or white fish, introduces necessary proteins without overwhelming the body with fats.

Beyond their nutritional benefits, soups and stews offer psychological comfort. The act of sitting down to a steamy bowl can be incredibly soothing, reminiscent of meals enjoyed in carefree days past. This emotional nourishment is crucial, as it interlinks with physical healing to propel recovery. In the earlier days post-surgery, when solid foods seem daunting, a silky butternut squash soup or a gentle lentil stew can be both appetizing and forgiving to the stomach.

Moreover, the ease of preparation makes soups and stews particularly appealing to those navigating post-surgery diets amidst busy schedules. A large pot of soup can be made in advance, providing several meals that require little more than reheating. This addresses not only the physical need for gentle nutrition but also the time management challenges that many face. The practicality of preparing a week's worth of meals in a single cooking session cannot be overstated; it simplifies diet management, ensuring adherence to nutritional guidelines without daily kitchen struggles.

Adaptation to a low-fat diet also involves relearning how to layer flavors without relying on fat as a primary carrier of taste. Herbs, spices, and aromatic vegetables become the culinary tools needed to build flavor. Imagine a tomato-based vegetable stew, wherein the acidity of tomatoes brightens the earthy tones of root vegetables and the sharpness of garlic and onions, all mellowed by a generous sprinkle of basil and oregano. Such a dish not only adheres to dietary needs but also delights the palate.

The therapeutic benefits of incorporating ingredients like ginger, turmeric, and fennel should also be considered. Known for their anti-inflammatory properties, these spices can aid digestion and alleviate some of the discomforts that come with gallbladder removal. Integrating these into soups and stews enhances their healing potential. For instance, a ginger-carrot soup not only provides a creamy texture and vibrant flavor but also offers gastrointestinal benefits that are much needed in a recovery diet.

The personalization of recipes is another aspect that can transform diet adaptation from a chore into a delightful exploration of new tastes. Experimenting with different ingredients allows individuals to cater to their unique preferences and tolerances, while still adhering to the critical low-fat requirement. Whether one leans towards the comforting simplicity of a vegetable puree or the robust heartiness of a bean stew, the key lies in crafting dishes that satisfy both the body's needs and the soul's cravings for comfort and flavor.

In closing, embracing low-fat soups and stews post-gallbladder surgery is not merely about adhering to dietary restrictions; it's about rediscovering the joy of eating through flavors that heal and nourish both body and spirit. Each spoonful should be a step towards recovery, packed with nutrients, infused with taste, and easy on the digestive system. As these meals become staples in the dietary routine, they pave the way to not only recovery but also a new understanding and enjoyment of food, crafted thoughtfully to support a healthier, gallbladder-free life.

ROASTED CARROT AND GINGER SOUP

PREPARATION TIME: 10 min - **COOKING TIME:** 30 min
MODE OF COOKING: Roasting and Blending - **SERVINGS:** 4
INGREDIENTS:

- 4 large carrots, peeled and chopped
- 1 onion, chopped
- 1-inch fresh ginger, peeled and sliced
- 1 Tbsp olive oil
- 4 cups vegetable broth

DIRECTIONS:

1. Preheat oven to 400°F (200°C).
2. Toss carrots, onion, and ginger with olive oil. Spread on a baking sheet.
3. Roast for 25 minutes until tender.
4. Transfer roasted vegetables to a blender, add vegetable broth, and blend until smooth.
5. Heat the soup in a pot until warmed through.

TIPS:

1. Garnish with fresh parsley or cilantro for added flavor.
2. Add a splash of coconut milk for creaminess.

N.V.:
Calories: 120, Fat: 3g, Carbs: 21g, Protein: 2g, Sugar: 9g, Cholesterol: 0mg

ZUCCHINI BASIL SOUP

PREPARATION TIME: 10 min - **COOKING TIME:** 20 min
MODE OF COOKING: Sautéing and Blending - **SERVINGS:** 4
INGREDIENTS:

- 4 zucchinis, chopped
- 1 onion, chopped
- 2 cups fresh basil leaves
- 1 Tbsp olive oil
- 4 cups vegetable broth

DIRECTIONS:

1. Heat olive oil in a large pot over medium heat.
2. Add chopped onion and sauté until translucent.
3. Add zucchini and cook until softened, about 10 minutes.
4. Add vegetable broth and bring to a simmer.
5. Transfer the mixture to a blender, add basil leaves, and blend until smooth.

TIPS:

1. Serve with a drizzle of olive oil and a sprinkle of black pepper.
2. For extra protein, add a spoonful of Greek yogurt.

N.V.:
Calories: 110, Fat: 4g, Carbs: 16g, Protein: 3g, Sugar: 8g, Cholesterol: 0mg

HEARTY LENTIL STEW

PREPARATION TIME: 10 min - **COOKING TIME:** 30 min
MODE OF COOKING: Simmering - **SERVINGS:** 4
INGREDIENTS:

- 1 cup green lentils, rinsed
- 1 onion, chopped
- 2 carrots, chopped
- 2 celery stalks, chopped
- 4 cups vegetable broth
- 1 tsp cumin
- 1 tsp smoked paprika

DIRECTIONS:

1. In a large pot, combine lentils, onion, carrots, and celery.
2. Add vegetable broth, cumin, and smoked paprika.
3. Bring to a boil, then reduce heat and simmer for 30 minutes until lentils are tender.

TIPS:

1. Add a squeeze of lemon juice before serving for a burst of freshness.
2. Garnish with fresh parsley for added flavor.

N.V.:
Calories: 180, Fat: 0.5g, Carbs: 32g, Protein: 12g, Sugar: 4g, Cholesterol: 0mg

SPICY BLACK BEAN STEW

PREPARATION TIME: 10 min - **COOKING TIME:** 20 min
MODE OF COOKING: Simmering - **SERVINGS:** 4
INGREDIENTS:

- 2 cups canned black beans, rinsed and drained
- 1 red bell pepper, chopped
- 1 onion, chopped
- 2 garlic cloves, minced
- 4 cups vegetable broth
- 1 tsp chili powder
- 1/2 tsp cumin

DIRECTIONS:

1. In a large pot, sauté onion, bell pepper, and garlic until softened.
2. Add black beans, vegetable broth, chili powder, and cumin.
3. Bring to a boil, then reduce heat and simmer for 20 minutes.

TIPS:

1. Top with avocado slices for a creamy texture.
2. Serve with a side of brown rice for a complete meal.

N.V.:
Calories: 150, Fat: 1g, Carbs: 25g, Protein: 7g, Sugar: 3g, Cholesterol: 0mg

CHICKEN AND VEGETABLE CLEAR BROTH

PREPARATION TIME: 10 min - **COOKING TIME:** 30 min
MODE OF COOKING: Simmering - **SERVINGS:** 4
INGREDIENTS:

- 1 boneless, skinless chicken breast
- 1 carrot, sliced
- 1 celery stalk, sliced
- 1 small onion, chopped
- 4 cups low-sodium chicken broth
- 1 bay leaf
- Salt and pepper to taste

DIRECTIONS:

1. In a pot, bring chicken broth to a boil.
2. Add chicken breast, carrot, celery, onion, and bay leaf.
3. Reduce heat and simmer for 30 minutes until chicken is cooked through.
4. Remove chicken, shred it, and return to the pot.
5. Season with salt and pepper.

TIPS:

1. Garnish with fresh parsley for added flavor.
2. Add a splash of lemon juice for brightness.

N.V.:
Calories: 90, Fat: 1g, Carbs: 6g, Protein: 14g, Sugar: 3g, Cholesterol: 30mg

TOFU AND SPINACH CLEAR BROTH

PREPARATION TIME: 5 min - **COOKING TIME:** 15 min
MODE OF COOKING: Simmering - **SERVINGS:** 4
INGREDIENTS:

- 1 cup firm tofu, cubed
- 4 cups vegetable broth
- 1 cup fresh spinach leaves
- 1 garlic clove, minced
- 1 tsp soy sauce
- Salt and pepper to taste

DIRECTIONS:

1. In a pot, bring vegetable broth to a boil.
2. Add tofu, garlic, and soy sauce.
3. Reduce heat and simmer for 10 minutes.
4. Add spinach and cook for an additional 5 minutes.
5. Season with salt and pepper.

TIPS:

1. Add a dash of sesame oil for extra flavor.
2. Serve with a side of brown rice for a complete meal.

N.V.:
Calories: 70, Fat: 2g, Carbs: 6g, Protein: 6g, Sugar: 1g, Cholesterol: 0mg

5.2 REFRESHING SALADS AND DRESSINGS

Stepping into your kitchen post-gallbladder surgery can be a transformative experience if you approach it with a spirit of innovation and mindfulness. Among the diverse range of meal options, salads stand out as a beacon of refreshment and nourishment. These delightful dishes not only cater to your digestive requirements but also open up a canvas for creativity. Let's delve into the art of crafting refreshing salads and dressing them in ways that keep your digestive health in check while tantalizing your taste buds.

Imagine a palette of greens laid out before you, each leafy vegetable promising a crunch that resonates with freshness and earthiness. The varieties are many: romaine's sturdy, crisp leaves; arugula's peppery bite; spinach's soft, iron-rich embrace. Each green offers unique nutrients and textures, serving as the perfect backdrop for a gamut of colorful additions.

When you think of adding proteins to your salad, consider the lean, gentle-on-the-stomach varieties. Grilled chicken breast, flaked salmon, or even a handful of chickpeas can turn your simple salad into a fulfilling meal that supports your nutritional needs without overwhelming your digestive system. The key here is to ensure these proteins are cooked using low-fat methods: grilling, baking, or poaching.

Navigating the world of dressings post-surgery can be akin to finding a new best friend who understands your needs and enhances your life. The high-fat, creamy dressage's that you may have savored before must now give way to lighter, zesty alternatives. Think of a freshly whisked vinaigrette with olive oil and lemon juice, seasoned with a touch of mustard for an emulsifying effect and herbs for flavor. Olive oil, in moderation, is your ally here, offering a healthy fat that aids in the absorption of fat-soluble vitamins without stressing your liver.

But let's not stop at vinaigrettes. Consider the tang of yogurt-based dressings—opt for Greek yogurt for its protein and probiotic boost—seasoned with herbs like dill or tarragon. The slight tartness of the yogurt complements the crispness of fresh vegetables beautifully, adding a creamy texture without the weight of traditional mayonnaise.

Creating a salad can be as simple as tossing together these elements, but let's elevate it by weaving in flavors and textures that surprise and delight. Add a crunch with slivered almonds or walnuts, remembering that nuts are also a good source of healthy fats important for your modified diet. Introduce sweetness with slices of apple or pear, or a handful of berries for a burst of antioxidants.

Edible flowers might also find a place in your new salad repertoire. Consider how a sprinkle of bright, peppery nasturtiums or the subtle sweetness of violets might not only beautify your dish but also elevate your mood and plate aesthetics.

As you adapt to this new way of crafting salads, you might find it helpful to maintain a small garden of fresh herbs and easy-to-grow greens. Having these ingredients at hand can inspire you to mix up a salad at a moment's notice, ensuring you have access to fresh, easy-to-digest meals that don't become repetitive.

Moreover, embracing the seasons can transform your salad experience entirely. Each season brings its bounty: the tender sprouts of spring, hearty leaves of summer, root vegetables in autumn, and even the storied squashes of winter. Rotate these through your salad creations to maintain an appealing variety and to take advantage of the freshest, most nutritious options available.

In practical terms, mastering the art of salad-making post-gallbladder removal isn't just about sticking to a diet plan; it's about re-engaging with food in a way that promotes healing and health. It requires you to sometimes think like a nutritionist, selecting ingredients for their digestive benefits, and other times like a chef, more focused on flavor and presentation.

Let each salad be an exploration, a small adventure on your plate. As you become more comfortable and confident in your choices, you'll find that these dishes provide both the physical nourishment your body needs and the psychological boost of knowing you're caring for yourself with every bite. Your journey through recovery can be vibrant and full of discovery, with each meal a step toward renewed health.

SPINACH AND BERRY DELIGHT WITH LEMON-HONEY DRESSING

PREPARATION TIME: 10 min - **COOKING TIME:** 0 min
MODE OF COOKING: Raw - **SERVINGS:** 4
INGREDIENTS:

- 4 cups baby spinach
- 1 cup fresh strawberries, sliced
- 1/2 cup blueberries
- 1/4 cup red onion, thinly sliced

Lemon-Honey Dressing:

- 2 Tbsp lemon juice
- 1 Tbsp honey
- 1 Tbsp olive oil
- Salt and pepper to taste

DIRECTIONS:

1. In a large bowl, combine spinach, strawberries, blueberries, and red onion.
2. In a small bowl, whisk together lemon juice, honey, olive oil, salt, and pepper.
3. Drizzle dressing over salad and toss gently to combine.

TIPS:

1. Add a sprinkle of feta cheese for extra flavor.
2. Toasted nuts can add a delightful crunch.

N.V.:
Calories: 80, Fat: 3g, Carbs: 12g, Protein: 1g, Sugar: 9g, Cholesterol: 0mg

MIXED GREENS WITH CUCUMBER AND YOGURT DILL DRESSING

PREPARATION TIME: 10 min - **COOKING TIME:** 0 min
MODE OF COOKING: Raw - **SERVINGS:** 4
INGREDIENTS:

- 4 cups mixed greens (lettuce, arugula, baby kale)
- 1 cucumber, thinly sliced
- 1/4 cup cherry tomatoes, halved

Yogurt Dill Dressing:

- 1/2 cup low-fat plain yogurt
- 1 Tbsp fresh dill, chopped
- 1 Tbsp lemon juice
- Salt and pepper to taste

DIRECTIONS:

1. In a large bowl, combine mixed greens, cucumber, and cherry tomatoes.
2. In a small bowl, whisk together yogurt, dill, lemon juice, salt, and pepper.
3. Drizzle dressing over salad and toss gently to combine.

TIPS:

1. Add a handful of croutons for a crunchy texture.
2. Use Greek yogurt for a creamier dressing.

N.V.:
Calories: 60, Fat: 1.5g, Carbs: 10g, Protein: 2g, Sugar: 5g, Cholesterol: 0mg

QUINOA AND CHICKPEA SALAD WITH LEMON-TAHINI DRESSING

PREPARATION TIME: 10 min - **COOKING TIME:** 15 min
MODE OF COOKING: Boiling - **SERVINGS:** 4
INGREDIENTS:

- 1 cup quinoa, rinsed
- 1 can chickpeas, rinsed and drained
- 1 cucumber, diced
- 1/4 cup red onion, finely chopped
- 1/4 cup fresh parsley, chopped

Lemon-Tahini Dressing:

- 2 Tbsp tahini
- 2 Tbsp lemon juice
- 1 Tbsp olive oil
- 1 tsp honey
- Salt and pepper to taste

DIRECTIONS:

1. Cook quinoa according to package instructions. Let cool.
2. In a large bowl, combine quinoa, chickpeas, cucumber, red onion, and parsley.
3. In a small bowl, whisk together tahini, lemon juice, olive oil, honey, salt, and pepper.
4. Drizzle dressing over salad and toss gently to combine.

TIPS:

1. Add a handful of cherry tomatoes for extra color and flavor.
2. Store in the fridge for an hour before serving to enhance the flavors.

N.V.:
Calories: 200, Fat: 6g, Carbs: 30g, Protein: 7g, Sugar: 4g, Cholesterol: 0mg

FARRO AND ROASTED VEGETABLE SALAD WITH BALSAMIC VINAIGRETTE

PREPARATION TIME: 15 min - **COOKING TIME:** 25 min
MODE OF COOKING: Boiling and Roasting - **SERVINGS:** 4

INGREDIENTS:
- 1 cup farro
- 1 red bell pepper, chopped
- 1 zucchini, chopped
- 1 red onion, chopped
- 2 Tbsp olive oil
- 1/4 cup feta cheese, crumbled

Balsamic Vinaigrette:
- 2 Tbsp balsamic vinegar
- 1 Tbsp olive oil
- 1 tsp Dijon mustard
- 1 tsp honey
- Salt and pepper to taste

DIRECTIONS:
1. Preheat oven to 400°F (200°C).
2. Toss bell pepper, zucchini, and onion with olive oil and spread on a baking sheet.
3. Roast vegetables for 20 minutes until tender.
4. Meanwhile, cook farro according to package instructions. Let cool.
5. In a large bowl, combine farro, roasted vegetables, and feta cheese.
6. In a small bowl, whisk together balsamic vinegar, olive oil, Dijon mustard, honey, salt, and pepper.
7. Drizzle vinaigrette over salad and toss gently to combine.

TIPS:
1. Add a handful of fresh arugula for a peppery bite.
2. Garnish with toasted pine nuts for added texture.

N.V.:
Calories: 230, Fat: 8g, Carbs: 34g, Protein: 6g, Sugar: 6g, Cholesterol: 5mg

---

GRILLED CHICKEN AND QUINOA SALAD WITH AVOCADO LIME DRESSING

PREPARATION TIME: 15 min - **COOKING TIME:** 20 min
MODE OF COOKING: Grilling and Boiling - **SERVINGS:** 4
INGREDIENTS:
- 1 cup quinoa, rinsed
- 2 boneless, skinless chicken breasts
- 1 avocado, diced
- 1 cup cherry tomatoes, halved
- 1/4 cup red onion, finely chopped

Avocado Lime Dressing:
- 1 avocado
- 2 Tbsp lime juice
- 1 Tbsp olive oil
- Salt and pepper to taste
-

DIRECTIONS:
1. Cook quinoa according to package instructions. Let cool.
2. Season chicken breasts with salt and pepper. Grill over medium heat for 6-7 minutes per side until cooked through. Let rest, then slice.
3. In a large bowl, combine quinoa, chicken, diced avocado, cherry tomatoes, and red onion.
4. In a blender, combine avocado, lime juice, olive oil, salt, and pepper. Blend until smooth.
5. Drizzle dressing over salad and toss gently to combine.

TIPS:
1. Add a handful of fresh cilantro for added flavor.
2. Use grilled shrimp instead of chicken for a variation.

N.V.:
Calories: 280, Fat: 12g, Carbs: 24g, Protein: 22g, Sugar: 2g, Cholesterol: 40mg

---

LENTIL AND SPINACH SALAD WITH LEMON GARLIC DRESSING

PREPARATION TIME: 10 min - **COOKING TIME:** 20 min
MODE OF COOKING: Boiling - **SERVINGS:** 4
INGREDIENTS:
- 1 cup green lentils, rinsed
- 4 cups baby spinach
- 1/2 cup cucumber, diced
- 1/4 cup red bell pepper, chopped

Lemon Garlic Dressing:
- 2 Tbsp lemon juice
- 1 Tbsp olive oil
- 1 garlic clove, minced
- Salt and pepper to taste

DIRECTIONS:
1. Cook lentils in boiling water until tender, about 20 minutes. Drain and let cool.
2. In a large bowl, combine lentils, spinach, cucumber, and red bell pepper.
3. In a small bowl, whisk together lemon juice, olive oil, garlic, salt, and pepper.
4. Drizzle dressing over salad and toss gently to combine.

TIPS:
1. Add crumbled feta cheese for extra flavor.

2. Garnish with toasted sunflower seeds for added crunch.

N.V.:
Calories: 220, Fat: 6g, Carbs: 32g, Protein: 12g, Sugar: 3g, Cholesterol: 0mg

5.3 SIMPLE SANDWICHES AND WRAPS

In the journey of adapting to life without a gallbladder, the midday meal often poses a unique set of challenges and opportunities. Lunch, nestled between the start of our day and the evening wind down, needs to be nourishing yet light enough to prevent digestive discomfort—a common concern for those who've undergone gallbladder removal. Here, I'll guide you through the craft of assembling simple sandwiches and wraps that are not just safe and soothing for your digestive system, but delicious and varied enough to bring joy and satisfaction to your lunchtime routine.

Imagine this: it's noon, and you're feeling the midday slump. You crave something that's both refreshing and fulfilling without the heaviness that could trigger discomfort. This is where the artistry of sandwich and wrap making truly shines. The beauty of these lunchtime staples lies in their versatility. You can adapt them to include a variety of low-fat, high-fiber ingredients that cater to a sensitive digestive system, ensuring each bite is as gentle as it is flavorful.

Starting with bread, the base of many great sandwiches, opt for whole-grain or sourdough options. These choices not only offer a richer flavor profile but also integrate the benefits of added fiber, which is crucial in aiding digestion, especially post-gallbladder surgery. The complex carbohydrates in whole grains provide a steady source of energy, keeping you fueled and focused throughout the afternoon.

For those who find traditional bread too heavy, wraps present a wonderful alternative. Look for wraps made from whole grains and enriched with superfoods like chia or flaxseeds. These not only enhance the nutritional value but also improve the texture and taste of your creations. When you build your wrap, think about the balance of ingredients—how the slight bitterness of greens melds with the sweetness of bell peppers or how the crunch of cucumber slices complements the softness of avocado.

Choosing the right fillings is critical, too. Lean proteins such as grilled chicken, turkey, or plant-based alternatives like tempeh provide the necessary building blocks for repair and maintenance of your body tissues without taxing your digestion. Accompany these with a spread of hummus or a drizzle of a yogurt-based dressing instead of the higher-fat mayonnaise or creamy sauces. Not only do these substitutes keep the fat content in check, but they also introduce a tangy or savory flavor that enhances the overall taste of your sandwich or wrap.

Incorporating a variety of vegetables adds both texture and valuable nutrients to your meal. Lettuce, arugula, and baby spinach offer a crisp freshness, while grated carrots or thin slices of radish add a peppery or sweet note. These vegetables are not just fillers; they are packed with vitamins and help increase your meal's fiber content, which is particularly beneficial for supporting digestion.

Herbs and spices, too, can transform your meal from ordinary to extraordinary. Fresh basil, cilantro, or parsley can bring a burst of freshness, while a pinch of cumin or coriander can add warmth and depth. The key is to use these flavor enhancers judiciously to enrich your meal without overwhelming the delicate balance needed for a post-surgical diet.

While enjoying these meals, it's crucial to eat mindfully—taking the time to chew thoroughly and appreciate the flavors and textures. Eating slowly not only enhances your culinary experience but also helps in breaking down the food more efficiently, making digestion smoother and more comfortable

TURKEY AVOCADO WHOLE GRAIN SANDWICH

PREPARATION TIME: 10 min - **COOKING TIME:** 0 min
MODE OF COOKING: Assembly - **SERVINGS:** 2
INGREDIENTS:

- 4 slices whole grain bread
- 4 oz sliced turkey breast
- 1 avocado, sliced
- 1 tomato, sliced
- 1 cup fresh spinach leaves

DIRECTIONS:

1. Lay out whole grain bread slices.
2. Layer turkey breast, avocado slices, tomato slices, and spinach leaves on two slices of bread.
3. Top with remaining bread slices.
4. Cut each sandwich in half and serve.

TIPS:

1. Add a spread of hummus for extra flavor.
2. Use whole grain mustard for a tangy kick.

N.V.:
Calories: 350, Fat: 15g, Carbs: 38g, Protein: 20g, Sugar: 4g, Cholesterol: 35mg

HUMMUS AND VEGGIE WHOLE GRAIN SANDWICH

PREPARATION TIME: 10 min - **COOKING TIME:** 0 min
MODE OF COOKING: Assembly - **SERVINGS:** 2
INGREDIENTS:

- 4 slices whole grain bread
- 1/2 cup hummus
- 1/2 cucumber, sliced
- 1/4 red bell pepper, sliced
- 1/4 cup shredded carrots
- 1 cup mixed greens

DIRECTIONS:

1. Spread hummus evenly on each slice of whole grain bread.
2. Layer cucumber slices, red bell pepper slices, shredded carrots, and mixed greens on two slices of bread.
3. Top with remaining bread slices.
4. Cut each sandwich in half and serve.

TIPS:

1. Add a sprinkle of feta cheese for extra tang.
2. Use a variety of colored bell peppers for a vibrant look.

N.V.:
Calories: 300, Fat: 8g, Carbs: 50g, Protein: 10g, Sugar: 5g, Cholesterol: 0mg

ASIAN CHICKEN LETTUCE WRAPS

PREPARATION TIME: 15 min - **COOKING TIME:** 10 min
MODE OF COOKING: Sautéing - **SERVINGS:** 4
INGREDIENTS:

- 1 lb ground chicken
- 1 Tbsp olive oil
- 2 cloves garlic, minced
- 1 small onion, finely chopped
- 1 red bell pepper, diced
- 1/4 cup hoisin sauce
- 1 Tbsp soy sauce (low sodium)
- 1 Tbsp rice vinegar
- 1 tsp ginger, grated
- 8 large lettuce leaves (Bibb or Romaine)

DIRECTIONS:

1. Heat olive oil in a large pan over medium-high heat.
2. Add garlic, onion, and ginger, sauté until fragrant.
3. Add ground chicken and cook until browned, breaking it up with a spoon.
4. Stir in bell pepper, hoisin sauce, soy sauce, and rice vinegar. Cook for another 2-3 minutes.
5. Spoon the chicken mixture into lettuce leaves.
6. Serve warm, folded like a taco.

TIPS:

1. Add a squeeze of lime for extra freshness.
2. Top with chopped peanuts or cilantro for added flavor.

N.V.: Calories: 190, Fat: 8g, Carbs: 9g, Protein: 22g, Sugar: 6g, Cholesterol: 65mg, Sodium: 560mg, Fiber: 1g

TURKEY AVOCADO LETTUCE WRAPS

PREPARATION TIME: 10 min - **COOKING TIME:** 0 min
MODE OF COOKING: No cooking required - **SERVINGS:** 4
INGREDIENTS:

- 8 large lettuce leaves (Iceberg or Romaine)
- 8 oz sliced turkey breast (low sodium)
- 1 avocado, sliced
- 1/2 cup cherry tomatoes, halved
- 1/4 cup red onion, thinly sliced
- 2 Tbsp low-fat mayonnaise or Greek yogurt
- 1 tsp Dijon mustard

DIRECTIONS:

1. In a small bowl, mix the mayonnaise (or yogurt) with Dijon mustard.
2. Lay the lettuce leaves flat and spread a thin layer of the mustard mixture on each.
3. Place slices of turkey, avocado, cherry tomatoes, and red onion on each lettuce leaf.
4. Roll the lettuce leaves tightly and secure with a toothpick if necessary.
5. Serve immediately.
6.

TIPS:

1. Add a sprinkle of black pepper or a dash of hot sauce for extra kick.
2. Use a variety of colorful vegetables for added nutrition and visual appeal.

N.V.: Calories: 150, Fat: 10g, Carbs: 6g, Protein: 12g, Sugar: 2g, Cholesterol: 35mg, Sodium: 370mg, Fiber: 4g

CREAMY AVOCADO AND GREEK YOGURT SPREAD

PREPARATION TIME: 10 min
COOKING TIME: None
MODE OF COOKING: No cooking required - **SERVINGS:** 4
INGREDIENTS:

- 1 ripe avocado
- 1/2 cup plain Greek yogurt (low-fat)
- 1 Tbsp lemon juice
- 1 clove garlic, minced
- Salt and pepper to taste

DIRECTIONS:

1. In a bowl, mash the avocado until smooth.
2. Stir in Greek yogurt, lemon juice, minced garlic, salt, and pepper.
3. Mix until well combined.
4. Serve immediately or store in the refrigerator for up to 2 days.

TIPS:

1. Add a dash of hot sauce for a spicy kick.
2. Spread on whole grain bread or use as a dip for veggies.

N.V.: Calories: 100, Fat: 7g, Carbs: 8g, Protein: 5g, Sugar: 2g, Cholesterol: 5mg, Sodium: 45mg, Fiber: 4g

HUMMUS WITH SUN-DRIED TOMATOES

PREPARATION TIME: 10 min
COOKING TIME: None
MODE OF COOKING: No cooking required - **SERVINGS:** 4
INGREDIENTS:

- 1 can (15 oz) chickpeas, drained and rinsed
- 2 Tbsp tahini
- 2 Tbsp lemon juice
- 2 cloves garlic, minced
- 1/4 cup sun-dried tomatoes, finely chopped
- 1/4 cup water
- Salt to taste

DIRECTIONS:

1. In a food processor, blend chickpeas, tahini, lemon juice, garlic, and water until smooth.
2. Stir in chopped sun-dried tomatoes.
3. Season with salt to taste.
4. Serve immediately or store in the refrigerator for up to 5 days.

TIPS: Add a sprinkle of paprika for extra flavor.

1. Use as a spread for sandwiches or a dip for pita bread.

N.V.: Calories: 130, Fat: 6g, Carbs: 16g, Protein: 5g, Sugar: 1g, Cholesterol: 0mg, Sodium: 140mg, Fiber: 4g

50

CHAPTER 6: DELICIOUS AND DIGESTIVE-FRIENDLY DINNERS

6.1 LEAN PROTEINS AND HEALTHY SIDES

When embarking on a journey to harmonize your menu with the needs of a digestive system adjusting to life without a gallbladder, understanding how to incorporate lean proteins and healthful sides is more than a meal preparation task—it's a step towards reclaiming the joys of eating without discomfort.

Lean proteins are an essential part of this adjustment because they are relatively easy to digest and do not impose the heavy burden that their fattier counterparts might. Chicken breast, fish like cod or tilapia, turkey, and even cuts of pork like tenderloin are prime examples of lean meats that can be beautifully incorporated into your meals without overwhelming your system. Plant-based proteins such as lentils, chickpeas, and a variety of beans also provide substantial nutrition without causing distress. They are supportive of your digestive health, offering both protein and fiber which help to moderate the digestive process.

Preparing these proteins in a manner that respects your body's adjusted way of handling fats is crucial. Grilling, poaching, broiling, or baking with a light touch of olive oil, or a wonderfully aromatic broth, allows these proteins to retain moisture and flavor while keeping the fat content in check. The use of herbs and spices like turmeric, ginger, and parsley not only enhances flavor but also offers anti-inflammatory benefits, which are particularly valuable in your culinary toolbox post-surgery.

Pairing these proteins with the right kinds of sides can turn a simple dish into a nourishing meal that supports your digestive health. The emphasis here is on foods that are not only gentle on the stomach but also beneficial in aiding a smooth digestive process. Vegetables that are steamed or roasted such as carrots, zucchini, bell peppers, and spinach offer nutrient-density without too much fiber, which can sometimes be harsh on a sensitive digestive system. Quinoa and brown rice are excellent grains that complement your protein choice by providing a satisfying texture and yet, they are easy enough on the digestion.

A delightful way to bring these elements together might be a dish of roasted cod seasoned with lemon and dill, served alongside quinoa tossed with a medley of lightly sautéed garlic, spinach, and cherry tomatoes. This meal isn't just easy to digest; it's also an invitation back to the pleasure of eating, assuring you that post-gallbladder life can still be both delicious and fulfilling.

In crafting meals that fit your new dietary needs, there is something quite profound in the act of choosing ingredients that align with both nourishment and digestibility. For instance, embracing the natural oils found in fish like salmon or trout, which are rich in omega-3 fatty acids, can actually aid your digestion and reduce inflammation. These kinds of integrative choices support not just your physical health but also your wellness and happiness around eating.

Moreover, it's vital to listen to your body as it may react differently to foods post-surgery. What works for one person might not suit another. This personalized journey can sometimes feel like navigating a new territory without a map. However, with patience and attentive observation, you will begin to discern which foods to embrace and which to limit. For example, while whole grains are encouraged, your body might initially handle them better when they are well-cooked or soaked.

As we talk about adopting and enjoying a diet rich in lean proteins and healthy sides, it's also important to discuss what to drink during meals. Fluids are crucial, but timing and choice of beverage can significantly influence your digestion. Drinking lightly flavored water or herbal teas like peppermint or chamomile can soothe your stomach during or after meals. On the other hand, it might be wise to minimize high-sugar or caffeinated drinks, which can disrupt digestion.

Lastly, while discussing the well-rounded approach to eating after gallbladder surgery, it's empowering to emphasize the freedom and creativity still very much at your disposal. With every herb sprinkled or vegetable chopped, there's an opportunity to redefine what healthy eating means to you now. Reinventing these mealtime traditions in ways that speak to both your palate and your physical needs can be a deeply satisfying experience, profoundly expressive of care and consideration you are extending to yourself.

Each meal you prepare is a step forward in your journey towards adapting to a gallbladder-free lifestyle, helping you move toward a life where food continues to be a source of comfort and joy rather than discomfort. Whether it's a plate of grilled chicken with a side of steamed broccoli or a bowl of lentil soup with a sprinkle of fresh cilantro, each dish is a testament to your resilience and adaptability—a celebration of both flavor and life after surgery.

LEMON HERB GRILLED CHICKEN

PREPARATION TIME: 10 min - **COOKING TIME:** 15 min
MODE OF COOKING: Grilling - **SERVINGS:** 4
INGREDIENTS:
- 4 boneless, skinless chicken breasts
- 2 Tbsp olive oil
- 2 Tbsp lemon juice
- 2 cloves garlic, minced
- 1 tsp dried oregano
- 1 tsp dried thyme
- Salt and pepper to taste

DIRECTIONS:
1. In a bowl, mix olive oil, lemon juice, garlic, oregano, thyme, salt, and pepper.
2. Coat the chicken breasts in the marinade. Let sit for at least 10 minutes.
3. Preheat grill to medium-high heat.
4. Grill chicken for 6-7 minutes per side, until fully cooked.
5. Serve warm with a squeeze of fresh lemon.

TIPS:
1. Marinate the chicken overnight for deeper flavor.
2. Serve with a side of steamed vegetables or a fresh salad.

N.V.: Calories: 220, Fat: 9g, Carbs: 1g, Protein: 32g, Sugar: 0g, Cholesterol: 85mg, Sodium: 120mg, Fiber: 0g

CITRUS HERB GRILLED FISH

PREPARATION TIME: 10 min - **COOKING TIME:** 10 min
MODE OF COOKING: Grilling - **SERVINGS:** 4

INGREDIENTS:
- 4 fillets of white fish (cod, tilapia, or halibut)
- 2 Tbsp olive oil
- 1 orange, juiced and zested
- 1 lemon, juiced and zested
- 1 tsp dried dill
- Salt and pepper to taste

DIRECTIONS:
1. In a small bowl, combine olive oil, orange juice, lemon juice, orange zest, lemon zest, dill, salt, and pepper.
2. Brush the mixture onto both sides of the fish fillets.
3. Preheat grill to medium heat.
4. Grill fish for 4-5 minutes on each side, until the fish is opaque and flakes easily with a fork.
5. Serve immediately with a garnish of fresh herbs.

TIPS:
1. Use fresh herbs like parsley or cilantro for added freshness.
2. Pair with a quinoa salad or grilled vegetables for a complete meal.

N.V.: Calories: 200, Fat: 8g, Carbs: 2g, Protein: 30g, Sugar: 1g, Cholesterol: 65mg, Sodium: 90mg, Fiber: 0g

LEMON GARLIC STEAMED BROCCOLI

PREPARATION TIME: 5 min - **COOKING TIME:** 10 min
MODE OF COOKING: Steaming - **SERVINGS:** 4
INGREDIENTS:
- 1 lb broccoli florets
- 2 cloves garlic, minced
- 1 Tbsp olive oil
- 1 lemon, juiced
- Salt and pepper to taste

DIRECTIONS:
1. Steam broccoli florets until tender, about 7-10 minutes.
2. In a small pan, heat olive oil over medium heat.
3. Add minced garlic and sauté until fragrant, about 1 minute.
4. Drizzle the garlic oil over the steamed broccoli.
5. Squeeze lemon juice over the top and season with salt and pepper.
6. Serve warm.

TIPS:

1. Add a sprinkle of red pepper flakes for a bit of heat.
2. Serve as a side to grilled chicken or fish.

N.V.: Calories: 70, Fat: 4g, Carbs: 7g, Protein: 2g, Sugar: 2g, Cholesterol: 0mg, Sodium: 30mg, Fiber: 3g

STEAMED CARROTS WITH HONEY AND GINGER

PREPARATION TIME: 5 min - **COOKING TIME:** 10 min

MODE OF COOKING: Steaming - **SERVINGS:** 4

INGREDIENTS:

- 1 lb carrots, peeled and sliced
- 1 Tbsp honey
- 1 tsp fresh ginger, grated
- 1 Tbsp olive oil
- Salt to taste

DIRECTIONS:

1. Steam carrot slices until tender, about 8-10 minutes.
2. In a small bowl, whisk together honey, grated ginger, and olive oil.
3. Toss the steamed carrots with the honey-ginger mixture.
4. Season with salt to taste.
5. Serve warm.

TIPS:

1. Garnish with chopped fresh parsley for added color and flavor.
2. Serve alongside a lean protein for a complete meal.

N.V.: Calories: 90, Fat: 4g, Carbs: 13g, Protein: 1g, Sugar: 8g, Cholesterol: 0mg, Sodium: 40mg, Fiber: 3g

LEMON HERB QUINOA

PREPARATION TIME: 5 min - **COOKING TIME:** 15 min

MODE OF COOKING: Boiling - **SERVINGS:** 4

INGREDIENTS:

- 1 cup quinoa, rinsed
- 2 cups water
- 1 lemon, zested and juiced
- 1 Tbsp olive oil
- 1 tsp dried thyme
- Salt and pepper to taste

DIRECTIONS:

1. In a medium saucepan, bring water to a boil.
2. Add quinoa, reduce heat to low, cover, and simmer for 15 minutes or until water is absorbed.
3. Remove from heat and fluff with a fork.
4. Stir in lemon zest, lemon juice, olive oil, thyme, salt, and pepper.
5. Serve warm.

TIPS:

1. Add chopped fresh parsley for extra flavor and color.
2. Serve as a side dish with grilled chicken or fish.

N.V.: Calories: 180, Fat: 6g, Carbs: 29g, Protein: 6g, Sugar: 1g, Cholesterol: 0mg, Sodium: 10mg, Fiber: 3g

BROWN RICE PILAF WITH VEGETABLES

PREPARATION TIME: 10 min - **COOKING TIME:** 30 min

MODE OF COOKING: Sautéing and Boiling - **SERVINGS:** 4

INGREDIENTS:

- 1 cup brown rice
- 2 cups vegetable broth
- 1 Tbsp olive oil
- 1 small onion, finely chopped
- 1 carrot, diced
- 1 celery stalk, diced
- 1/2 cup peas
- Salt and pepper to taste

DIRECTIONS:

1. In a large pan, heat olive oil over medium heat.
2. Sauté onion, carrot, and celery until tender, about 5 minutes.
3. Add brown rice and cook, stirring frequently, for 2-3 minutes.
4. Add vegetable broth, bring to a boil, then reduce heat to low.
5. Cover and simmer for 30 minutes or until rice is tender and liquid is absorbed.
6. Stir in peas, and season with salt and pepper.
7. Serve warm.

TIPS:

1. Add a dash of soy sauce for an umami boost.
2. Serve with a side of steamed vegetables for a complete meal.

N.V.: Calories: 210, Fat: 5g, Carbs: 38g, Protein: 5g, Sugar: 3g, Cholesterol: 0mg, Sodium: 200mg, Fiber: 4g

Imagine coming home after a long day, yearning for comfort foods that once formed the centerpiece of family dinners or solitary indulgences after tough days. Yet now, post-gallbladder surgery, the thought of indulging in a rich, creamy pasta or a slice of savory pie fills you with hesitation. The good news? Comfort foods aren't off the menu; they just require a creative, health-conscious twist to align with your new dietary needs.

Traditionally, comfort food conjures images of hearty portions teeming with flavor and nostalgia. However, these dishes often come loaded with fats that can be challenging to digest for those without a gallbladder. The role of the gallbladder was to store bile, which helps in the digestion of fats. Without this storage mechanism, bile is released directly from the liver into the small intestine in a more constant, yet less concentrated flow, which can be less effective when dealing with large amounts of fat at once. This shift necessitates modifications to your diet, primarily reducing fat intake, which might seem like it would strip all the joy and flavor from your meals. But with a few adjustments, you can still embrace the warmth and comfort of your favorite foods.

Reimagining Pasta Dishes

One of the quintessential comfort foods is pasta. Full of carbs and typically coated in rich sauces, traditional pasta dishes might pose a problem due to their high-fat content, especially if they involve cream-based sauces or a generous topping of cheese. Instead, consider pasta made from whole grains or legumes, which offer more fiber and help support digestion. For the sauces, why not switch out heavy creams for pureed vegetables? A silky sauce made from pureed cauliflower or butternut squash, seasoned well with herbs and spices, can be just as satisfying but much gentler on your system. Adding in aromatic herbs like basil, oregano, or thyme can elevate the flavors. You can also incorporate lean proteins such as grilled chicken strips or white fish pieces to keep the meal balanced and satisfying.

Crafting Healthier Casseroles

Casseroles have always been a popular comfort food, likely because they remind us of family gatherings and festive celebrations. The traditional casserole, laden with cheese and creamy layers, might now be more of a challenge to digest. However, a reimagined casserole that uses layered roasted vegetables, a sprinkle of low-fat cheese, and lean meat such as turkey or chicken can fulfill that craving for something hearty without causing discomfort.

An innovative approach could include layering thinly sliced sweet potatoes, zucchini, and eggplant with some marinara sauce and shredded chicken. Top it with a light sprinkle of reduced-fat cheese. This version not only cuts down on fat but also increases the nutrient content with fiber-rich vegetables.

Refining the Art of Soups

Soup is comfort in a bowl, perfect for almost any occasion. Instead of cream-laden options, why not explore the rich, deep flavors that can be achieved with broths? Utilizing herbs, spices, and umami-rich ingredients like mushrooms or small amounts of parmesan can add layers of flavor without relying on fat.

A broth-based chicken soup with plenty of vegetables, barley, or even a bit of wild rice can be both filling and soothing. Adding herbs such as parsley, dill, or cilantro just before serving enhances the taste and brings freshness to each spoonful. Moreover, these ingredients stimulate digestion and enhance nutrient absorption, making each meal both medicinal and comforting.

Enjoying Gentle, Flavorful Innovation

In this era of culinary creativity, there are vast opportunities to modify traditional comfort foods into dishes that are both digestible and delightful. Techniques such as roasting, steaming, and poaching can bring out natural flavors and textures without the need for excessive fats.

Consider a shepherd's pie with a topping of mashed cauliflower mixed with a touch of olive oil instead of butter, or a mince filling made from turkey or lean beef, seasoned richly with onions, carrots, and peas. Likewise, fish pie can get a refreshing twist with a sweet potato crust and a filling enriched with leeks and fennel to boost its flavor profile without adding fat.

Nurturing a Relationship with Food

Adjusting to life without a gallbladder is not just about managing symptoms but also about rekindling a positive relationship with food. It's about recognizing that food can still bring comfort and joy, even when certain ingredients are off the table. It's also a time to explore new tastes and textures, to appreciate the natural flavors of high-quality ingredients, and to creatively use spices and herbs.

SPINACH AND TOMATO PASTA

PREPARATION TIME: 10 min - **COOKING TIME:** 20 min
MODE OF COOKING: Boiling and Sautéing - **SERVINGS:** 4
INGREDIENTS:

- 8 oz whole wheat pasta
- 1 Tbsp olive oil
- 2 cloves garlic, minced
- 1-pint cherry tomatoes, halved
- 4 cups fresh spinach
- Salt and pepper to taste
- 1/4 cup grated Parmesan cheese (optional)

DIRECTIONS:

1. Cook pasta according to package instructions. Drain and set aside.
2. In a large pan, heat olive oil over medium heat.
3. Add garlic and sauté until fragrant, about 1 minute.
4. Add cherry tomatoes and cook until softened, about 5 minutes.
5. Stir in spinach and cook until wilted, about 2-3 minutes.
6. Toss in the cooked pasta and mix until well combined.
7. Season with salt and pepper. Sprinkle with Parmesan cheese if desired.
8. Serve warm.

TIPS:

1. Add red pepper flakes for a spicy kick.
2. Use baby kale or arugula as a spinach substitute.

N.V.: Calories: 250, Fat: 7g, Carbs: 40g, Protein: 10g, Sugar: 4g, Cholesterol: 0mg, Sodium: 120mg, Fiber: 7g

LEMON GARLIC SHRIMP PASTA

PREPARATION TIME: 10 min - **COOKING TIME:** 15 min
MODE OF COOKING: Boiling and Sautéing - **SERVINGS:** 4
INGREDIENTS:

- 8 oz whole wheat pasta
- 1 lb large shrimp, peeled and deveined
- 1 Tbsp olive oil
- 3 cloves garlic, minced
- 1 lemon, juiced and zested
- 1/4 cup fresh parsley, chopped
- Salt and pepper to taste

DIRECTIONS:

1. Cook pasta according to package instructions. Drain and set aside.
2. In a large pan, heat olive oil over medium heat.
3. Add garlic and sauté until fragrant, about 1 minute.
4. Add shrimp and cook until pink and opaque, about 3-4 minutes per side.
5. Stir in lemon juice, lemon zest, and parsley.
6. Toss in the cooked pasta and mix until well combined.
7. Season with salt and pepper.
8. Serve warm.
9.

TIPS:

1. Add a pinch of red pepper flakes for heat.
2. Serve with a side of steamed vegetables for a complete meal.

N.V.: Calories: 280, Fat: 8g, Carbs: 35g, Protein: 25g, Sugar: 2g, Cholesterol: 180mg, Sodium: 220mg, Fiber: 6g

BROCCOLI AND CAULIFLOWER CASSEROLE

PREPARATION TIME: 15 min - **COOKING TIME:** 25 min
MODE OF COOKING: Baking - **SERVINGS:** 4
INGREDIENTS:

- 2 cups broccoli florets
- 2 cups cauliflower florets
- 1 cup low-fat Greek yogurt
- 1/2 cup shredded low-fat cheddar cheese
- 1 clove garlic, minced
- 1 tsp dried thyme
- Salt and pepper to taste

DIRECTIONS:

1. Preheat oven to 375°F (190°C).
2. Steam broccoli and cauliflower until tender, about 5 minutes. Drain and set aside.
3. In a large bowl, mix Greek yogurt, cheddar cheese, garlic, thyme, salt, and pepper.
4. Add steamed broccoli and cauliflower to the bowl and mix until well coated.
5. Transfer the mixture to a baking dish.
6. Bake for 20 minutes, until the top is golden and bubbly.
7. Serve warm.

TIPS:

1. Add a sprinkle of paprika for extra flavor.
2. Use a mixture of your favorite cheeses for a different taste.

N.V.: Calories: 150, Fat: 5g, Carbs: 14g, Protein: 12g, Sugar: 4g, Cholesterol: 15mg, Sodium: 200mg, Fiber: 4g

SPINACH AND MUSHROOM QUINOA CASSEROLE

PREPARATION TIME: 15 min - **COOKING TIME:** 30 min
MODE OF COOKING: Baking - **SERVINGS:** 4
INGREDIENTS:

- 1 cup quinoa, rinsed
- 2 cups vegetable broth
- 2 cups fresh spinach, chopped
- 1 cup mushrooms, sliced
- 1/2 cup low-fat mozzarella cheese, shredded
- 1/4 cup low-fat Greek yogurt
- 1 tsp dried oregano
- Salt and pepper to taste

DIRECTIONS:

1. Preheat oven to 375°F (190°C).
2. Cook quinoa in vegetable broth according to package instructions. Set aside.
3. In a large bowl, mix cooked quinoa, spinach, mushrooms, mozzarella cheese, Greek yogurt, oregano, salt, and pepper.
4. Transfer the mixture to a baking dish.
5. Bake for 25-30 minutes, until the top is golden and the casserole is heated through.
6. Serve warm.

TIPS:

1. Add diced tomatoes for a burst of freshness.
2. Top with a sprinkle of Parmesan cheese for extra flavor.

N.V.: Calories: 220, Fat: 6g, Carbs: 32g, Protein: 12g, Sugar: 3g, Cholesterol: 10mg, Sodium: 180mg, Fiber: 5g

HEARTY CHICKEN AND BARLEY SOUP

PREPARATION TIME: 10 min - **COOKING TIME:** 40 min
MODE OF COOKING: Stovetop - **SERVINGS:** 4
INGREDIENTS:

- 1 lb diced chicken breast
- 1 cup pearl barley
- 2 carrots, 2 celery stalks, diced
- 1 onion, minced
- 8 cups chicken broth

PROCEDURE:

1. Sauté onion, carrots, and celery in a large pot until softened, about 5 minutes.
2. Add chicken and cook until browned.
3. Stir in barley, salt, and pepper.
4. Pour in broth, bring to a boil, then simmer for 30 minutes.

TIPS:

1. Add lemon juice before serving.
2. Toss in spinach or kale in the last 5 minutes.
3. Use pre-cooked chicken for convenience.

NUTRITIONAL VALUES:
Calories: 320, Fat: 4g, Carbs: 48g, Protein: 28g, Sugar: 4g, Cholesterol: 65mg, Sodium: 550mg, Fiber: 8g

CREAMY CAULIFLOWER AND LEEK SOUP

PREPARATION TIME: 10 min - **COOKING TIME:** 30 min
MODE OF COOKING: Stovetop - **SERVINGS:** 4
INGREDIENTS:

- 1 large cauliflower, chopped
- 2 leeks, sliced
- 4 cups vegetable broth
- 1 cup almond milk

PROCEDURE:

1. Sauté leeks in a large pot until softened, about 5 minutes.
2. Add cauliflower, salt, and pepper, cook for 2 minutes.
3. Pour in broth, bring to a boil, then simmer for 20 minutes.
4. Puree the soup until smooth and stir in almond milk.

TIPS:

1. Garnish with chives or parsley.
2. Serve with whole-grain bread.
3. Add a pinch of nutmeg for warmth.

NUTRITIONAL VALUES:
Calories: 160, Fat: 4g, Carbs: 25g, Protein: 6g, Sugar: 7g, Cholesterol: 0mg, Sodium: 450mg, Fiber: 5g

6.3 ONE-POT MEALS AND CASSEROLES

In the journey of adapting to life without a gallbladder, mastering the art of creating one-pot meals and casseroles can be like finding a secret path through a dense forest. These cooking methods not only streamline the kitchen routine but also nurture the body with dishes that are gentle on the digestive system, full of flavor, and wonderfully satisfying.

Imagine a chilly evening when the thought of spending hours in the kitchen feels overwhelming. This is where the magic of one-pot meals comes to the rescue. With a single vessel, be it a pot, skillet, or slow cooker, you can conjure up a complete meal that harmonizes protein, veggies, and grains in a symphony of flavors, cooking together slowly, allowing their flavors to meld beautifully. This method is not only convenient but also cuts down on the washing up, allowing more time to unwind and enjoy the comfort of a nourishing meal.

Casseroles have a similar charm. They often remind us of family gatherings, a table bursting with laughter and stories, and a baking dish brimming with something delicious at the center. The beauty of passerines lies in their versatility and the ease with which they adapt to dietary needs. Post-gallbladder removal, the focus shifts prominently towards dishes that are low in fat and rich in fiber, and casseroles can be tailored precisely to fit this requirement.

In creating a one-pot meal or casserole, the first step is to choose ingredients that are both flavorful and kind to your digestive system. Lean proteins like chicken or turkey breast, fish, or tofu serve as excellent bases. They are easy on the stomach and rich in essential nutrients that aid in recovery and overall health. When it comes to vegetables, the variety is endless. From zucchini and carrots, which become wonderfully tender and sweet upon slow cooking, to leafy greens like kale and spinach, which add a pop of color and a boost of vitamins, your choices are plentiful.

The strategic use of herbs and spices plays a pivotal role here. Post-surgery diets often shy away from heavy use of fats for flavoring. Instead, herbs and spices can impart depth and complexity to dishes without adding any strain on digestion. Turmeric, with its anti-inflammatory properties, ginger, which aids in digestion, and herbs like basil and thyme, not only enhance flavor but also contribute health benefits.

The method of layering these ingredients is what transforms simple components into a comforting meal. In a casserole, for example, starting with a layer of sliced potatoes or whole-grain pasta, followed by a mix of sautéed vegetables, and topped with a protein, ensures that every bite is balanced. The use of vegetable broths or a splash of wine can add moisture and an extra dimension of flavor, which gently permeates the dish during the slow cooking process.

SKILLET LEMON HERB CHICKEN

PREPARATION TIME: 10 min - **COOKING TIME:** 20 min
MODE OF COOKING: Skillet - **SERVINGS:** 4

INGREDIENTS:
- 4 boneless, skinless chicken breasts
- 2 Tbsp olive oil
- 1 lemon, juiced
- 2 tsp dried oregano

PROCEDURE:
1. Heat olive oil in a large skillet over medium-high heat.
2. Add chicken breasts and cook until browned, about 5 minutes per side.
3. Pour lemon juice over chicken and sprinkle with oregano.
4. Reduce heat to medium and cook until chicken is fully cooked, about 10 minutes.

TIPS:
1. Garnish with lemon slices and fresh parsley for added flavor.
2. Serve with a side of steamed vegetables or quinoa.

NUTRITIONAL VALUES:
Calories: 280, Fat: 12g, Carbs: 2g, Protein: 38g, Sugar: 0g, Cholesterol: 100mg, Sodium: 75mg

VEGGIE-PACKED SKILLET QUINOA

PREPARATION TIME: 10 min - **COOKING TIME:** 20 min
MODE OF COOKING: Skillet - **SERVINGS:** 4
INGREDIENTS:
- 1 cup quinoa, rinsed
- 2 cups low-sodium vegetable broth
- 1 zucchini, diced
- 1 red bell pepper, diced

PROCEDURE:
1. In a large skillet, bring vegetable broth to a boil.
2. Add quinoa, reduce heat, cover, and simmer for 15 minutes.
3. Stir in zucchini and red bell pepper, and cook for an additional 5 minutes until vegetables are tender.

TIPS:

1. Add a sprinkle of feta cheese for extra flavor.
2. Mix in fresh spinach just before serving for added nutrients.

NUTRITIONAL VALUES:

Calories: 220, Fat: 4g, Carbs: 38g, Protein: 8g, Sugar: 4g, Cholesterol: 0mg, Sodium: 200mg

SLOW COOKER CHICKEN AND VEGETABLE STEW

PREPARATION TIME: 15 min - **COOKING TIME:** 6 hr
MODE OF COOKING: Slow Cooker - **SERVINGS:** 4
INGREDIENTS:

- 1 lb boneless, skinless chicken thighs, cubed
- 3 carrots, sliced
- 2 potatoes, diced
- 1 onion, chopped
- 4 cups low-sodium chicken broth

PROCEDURE:

1. Place chicken, carrots, potatoes, and onion into the slow cooker.
2. Pour in chicken broth and season with salt and pepper.
3. Cover and cook on low for 6 hours, until chicken is tender.

TIPS:

1. Add a bay leaf for extra flavor.
2. Stir in fresh spinach during the last 30 minutes of cooking.

NUTRITIONAL VALUES:

Calories: 250, Fat: 5g, Carbs: 30g, Protein: 22g, Sugar: 6g, Cholesterol: 70mg, Sodium: 400mg

SLOW COOKER LENTIL SOUP

PREPARATION TIME: 10 min - **COOKING TIME:** 6 hr
MODE OF COOKING: Slow Cooker - **SERVINGS:** 4
INGREDIENTS:

- 1 cup dried lentils, rinsed
- 2 carrots, diced
- 2 celery stalks, diced
- 1 onion, chopped
- 4 cups low-sodium vegetable broth

PROCEDURE:

1. Add lentils, carrots, celery, and onion to the slow cooker.
2. Pour in vegetable broth and stir to combine.

3. Cover and cook on low for 6 hours, until lentils are tender.
4.

TIPS:

1. Add a splash of lemon juice before serving for a fresh taste.
2. Garnish with chopped parsley for added color and flavor.
3.

NUTRITIONAL VALUES:

Calories: 180, Fat: 1g, Carbs: 35g, Protein: 12g, Sugar: 5g, Cholesterol: 0mg, Sodium: 300mg

ONE-POT LEMON HERB SALMON

PREPARATION TIME: 10 min - **COOKING TIME:** 20 min
MODE OF COOKING: Stovetop - **SERVINGS:** 4
INGREDIENTS:

- 4 salmon fillets
- 1 lemon, thinly sliced
- 2 Tbsp olive oil
- 1 tsp dried dill

PROCEDURE:

1. Heat olive oil in a large skillet over medium heat.
2. Place salmon fillets in the skillet and cook for 5 minutes.
3. Flip salmon, add lemon slices, and sprinkle with dill.
4. Cover and cook for another 15 minutes, until salmon is cooked through.

TIPS:

1. Serve with a side of steamed broccoli or asparagus.
2. Add a pinch of red pepper flakes for a bit of heat.

NUTRITIONAL VALUES:

Calories: 290, Fat: 18g, Carbs: 2g, Protein: 29g, Sugar: 0g, Cholesterol: 75mg, Sodium: 60mg

ONE-POT CHICKEN AND RICE

PREPARATION TIME: 10 min - **COOKING TIME:** 30 min
MODE OF COOKING: Stovetop - **SERVINGS:** 4
INGREDIENTS:

- 4 boneless, skinless chicken thighs
- 1 cup brown rice
- 2 cups low-sodium chicken broth
- 1 onion, chopped

PROCEDURE:

1. In a large pot, sauté onion until softened.

2. Add chicken thighs and brown on all sides.
3. Stir in rice and pour in chicken broth.
4. Bring to a boil, reduce heat, cover, and simmer for 30 minutes, until rice is tender and chicken is cooked through.

TIPS:

1. Add a handful of frozen peas in the last 5 minutes of cooking.
2. Garnish with chopped parsley for a fresh touch.

NUTRITIONAL VALUES:

Calories: 350, Fat: 10g, Carbs: 45g, Protein: 25g, Sugar: 2g, Cholesterol: 70mg, Sodium: 400mg

CHAPTER 7: SNACKS AND SMALL BITES

7.1 NUTRITIOUS ON-THE-GO SNACKS

In the bustling rhythm of day-to-day life, finding the right snack can sometimes feel like solving a particularly tricky puzzle. Post-gallbladder surgery, this challenge often intensifies, not just in choosing what to eat, but in ensuring these choices support your digestive health without forsaking flavor or convenience. Embracing a lifestyle with nutritious on-the-go snacks can be a joyful discovery rather than a dietary limitation.

Imagine this: it's mid-afternoon, you're running between meetings or just picking up the kids from school, and hunger strikes. This is the moment when having a smart, healthful snack handy can make all the difference in maintaining your energy levels and taking care of your digestion. The key is to select foods that are gentle on your system, easy to digest, and capable of giving you a much-needed boost without too much dietary fat, which is particularly crucial in a diet for those without a gallbladder.

One might wonder, "What makes a snack both gentle and nutritious?" It's about focusing on balance and simplicity. Foods rich in fiber, low in fats, and packed with nutrition are your best allies. Let's talk about some ingredients that fit this profile beautifully. Take nuts, for example, especially almonds, which are not only packed with protein but are also a good source of fiber. However, moderation is key, as nuts are also high in fats, albeit healthy ones. A small, palm-sized amount can provide enough energy without overwhelming your digestive system.

Pairing these with dried fruits can offer a sweet counterbalance that not only satisfies the taste buds but also infuses your body with natural sugars for energy. However, it's important to select unsweetened dried fruits to avoid excessive sugar intake. Together, nuts and dried fruits can keep your energy up and your digestion smooth without any fuss, perfect for those busy days.

Now, consider the versatility of seeds — pumpkin, sunflower, or chia seeds are fantastic options. These tiny powerhouses can be tossed into homemade trail mixes or sprinkled onto a low-fat yogurt, providing crunch and nutrients without a lot of effort. Seeds are a great source of fiber which aids in digestion and helps to regulate blood sugar levels, keeping those post-snack energy crashes at bay.

Speaking of yogurt, Greek yogurt, particularly those that are low in fat and high in live probiotics, can be an excellent snack for enhancing digestive health. Top it with a bit of honey and a sprinkle of your homemade seed mix, and you have a delightful, creamy snack that supports your dietary needs and keeps your taste buds happy.

Another wonderful snack option is hummus, chiefly made from chickpeas which are naturally high in protein and fiber but low in fat. This makes them ideal for someone managing life post-gallbladder removal. Pair hummus with raw veggies like carrot sticks, bell peppers, or cucumber slices for a satisfying crunch without any strain on your digestion.

For a change, why not turn to popcorn? Yes, when prepared healthily — without butter or excessive salt — popcorn can be a fantastic low-calorie, high-fiber snack that keeps you full and satisfied between meals. It's also a snack you can have a little fun with — try sprinkling a pinch of nutritional yeast or a dash of smoked paprika for a boost of flavor without added fats.

As the seasons turn colder, you might want to reach for something warm. Soup can be a comforting and nourishing snack, especially when made from scratch with fresh, low-fat ingredients. A clear broth with a mix of leafy greens, garlic, ginger, and some lean protein can be both restorative and easy to digest. Imagine sipping on a warm cup of homemade broth while reading your favorite book or winding down from a busy day. It's not only nourishing for the body but also soothing for the soul.

What's wonderful about these snack options is not just their nutritional profile but how seamlessly they can integrate into your lifestyle. Each can be prepared in advance, which is a boon for time management. Spending a Sunday afternoon prepping your snacks for the week can mean you're ready to grab and go when life accelerates to its weekday pace.

Further enhancing your snack arsenal could involve embracing the art of baking — think muffins, but with a twist. Using applesauce instead of butter, whole grain flours instead of refined ones, and adding in fruits like blueberries or rapids for their antioxidants, you can bake up delicious treats that won't strain your digestive system.

Navigating life post-gallbladder surgery with a mindful approach to snacking can effectively turn a dietary challenge into an exploration of tastes and textures that not only satisfy hunger but also support long-term health and wellness. It's about making informed choices, understanding the nutritional content, and most importantly, finding joy in the snacks you eat. This way, each bite not only nourishes your body but also brings a small moment of pleasure to your day, making the journey of recovery a path filled with delightful discoveries.

TROPICAL ENERGY BARS

PREPARATION TIME: 10 min. - **COOKING TIME:** 10 min.
MODE OF COOKING: Baking - **SERVINGS:** 8
INGREDIENTS:
- 1 cup rolled oats
- 1/2 cup dried mango, chopped
- 1/2 cup unsweetened shredded coconut
- 1/4 cup honey
- 1/4 cup almond butter

PROCEDURE:
1. Preheat oven to 350°F (175°C).
2. In a bowl, mix oats, dried mango, and shredded coconut.
3. In a small saucepan, warm honey and almond butter over low heat until smooth.
4. Pour the honey-almond butter mixture over the dry ingredients and stir until well combined.
5. Press the mixture into a lined 8x8 inch baking pan.
6. Bake for 10 minutes until lightly golden.
7. Cool completely before cutting into bars.

TIPS:
1. Add a tablespoon of chia seeds for extra fiber.
2. Substitute dried mango with dried pineapple for a different tropical twist.

NUTRITIONAL VALUES:
Calories: 150, Fat: 6g, Carbs: 22g, Protein: 3g, Sugar: 10g, Cholesterol: 0mg

ALMOND APRICOT ENERGY BARS

PREPARATION TIME: 15 min. - **COOKING TIME:** 10 min.
MODE OF COOKING: Baking - **SERVINGS:** 8
INGREDIENTS:
- 1 cup rolled oats
- 1/2 cup dried apricots, chopped
- 1/4 cup sliced almonds
- 1/4 cup honey
- 1/4 cup almond butter

PROCEDURE:
1. Preheat oven to 350°F (175°C).
2. In a bowl, mix oats, dried apricots, and sliced almonds.
3. In a small saucepan, warm honey and almond butter over low heat until smooth.
4. Pour the honey-almond butter mixture over the dry ingredients and stir until well combined.
5. Press the mixture into a lined 8x8 inch baking pan.
6. Bake for 10 minutes until lightly golden.
7. Cool completely before cutting into bars.

TIPS:
1. Add a teaspoon of vanilla extract for added flavor.
2. Store bars in the refrigerator to keep them fresh longer.

NUTRITIONAL VALUES:
Calories: 160, Fat: 7g, Carbs: 24g, Protein: 4g, Sugar: 11g, Cholesterol: 0mg

CLASSIC NUTS AND FRUIT TRAIL MIX

PREPARATION TIME: 5 min. - **COOKING TIME:** None
MODE OF COOKING: None - **SERVINGS:** 10
INGREDIENTS:
- 1 cup almonds
- 1 cup cashews
- 1 cup dried cranberries
- 1 cup raisins

PROCEDURE:
1. Combine all ingredients in a large bowl.
2. Mix well until evenly distributed.
3. Store in an airtight container.

TIPS:
1. Add a handful of sunflower seeds for extra crunch.
2. For a touch of sweetness, mix in a few dark chocolate chips.

NUTRITIONAL VALUES:
Calories: 200, Fat: 12g, Carbs: 22g, Protein: 4g, Sugar: 15g, Cholesterol: 0mg

TROPICAL TRAIL MIX

PREPARATION TIME: 5 min. - **COOKING TIME:** None
MODE OF COOKING: None - **SERVINGS:** 10
INGREDIENTS:
- 1 cup dried pineapple chunks

- 1 cup dried mango pieces
- 1 cup unsweetened coconut flakes
- 1 cup macadamia nuts

PROCEDURE:
1. Combine all ingredients in a large bowl.
2. Mix well until evenly distributed.
3. Store in an airtight container.

TIPS:
1. Add a few tablespoons of chia seeds for added nutrition.
2. Keep in a cool, dry place to maintain freshness.

NUTRITIONAL VALUES:
Calories: 210, Fat: 13g, Carbs: 24g, Protein: 2g, Sugar: 18g, Cholesterol: 0mg

CLASSIC VEGGIE STICKS WITH HUMMUS

PREPARATION TIME: 10 min. - **COOKING TIME:** None
MODE OF COOKING: None - **SERVINGS:** 4
INGREDIENTS:
- 2 carrots, cut into sticks
- 2 celery stalks, cut into sticks
- 1 cucumber, cut into sticks
- 1 cup store-bought hummus

PROCEDURE:
1. Arrange carrot, celery, and cucumber sticks on a serving plate.
2. Place hummus in a small bowl.
3. Serve veggies with hummus for dipping.

TIPS:
1. Add bell pepper sticks for more variety.
2. Sprinkle a dash of paprika on the hummus for extra flavor.

NUTRITIONAL VALUES:
Calories: 150, Fat: 8g, Carbs: 15g, Protein: 4g, Sugar: 4g, Cholesterol: 0mg

COLORFUL VEGGIE STICKS WITH HOMEMADE HUMMUS

PREPARATION TIME: 15 min. - **COOKING TIME:** None
MODE OF COOKING: None - **SERVINGS:** 4
INGREDIENTS:
- 1 red bell pepper, cut into sticks
- 1 yellow bell pepper, cut into sticks
- 2 carrots, cut into sticks
- 1 cucumber, cut into sticks
- 1 can chickpeas, drained and rinsed
- 2 Tbsp tahini
- 2 Tbsp lemon juice
- 1 clove garlic, minced
- 2 Tbsp water
- Salt to taste

PROCEDURE:
1. In a food processor, combine chickpeas, tahini, lemon juice, garlic, water, and salt.
2. Blend until smooth, adding more water if needed.
3. Arrange bell pepper, carrot, and cucumber sticks on a serving plate.
4. Serve homemade hummus in a bowl alongside the veggie sticks.

TIPS:
1. Add a drizzle of olive oil on top of the hummus for a richer taste.
2. Experiment with different vegetables like zucchini or jicama.

NUTRITIONAL VALUES:
Calories: 170, Fat: 7g, Carbs: 20g, Protein: 5g, Sugar: 6g, Cholesterol: 0mg

7.2 LOW-FAT DIPS AND SPREADS

Imagine walking into your kitchen on a quiet afternoon. The sun casts a warm glow through the windows, and you're inspired to whip up something light yet satisfying. This is where the magic of low-fat dips and spreads comes into play, transforming simple ingredients into culinary delights that are not only easy on your digestive system post-gallbladder surgery but also incredibly tasty.

Low-fat dips and spreads are versatile kitchen champions that can turn everyday snacks into a flavorful feast without overwhelming your digestive tract. The beauty of these condiments lies not only in their nutritional benefits but also in their ease of preparation and the joy of customization.

Let's start with understanding why low-fat options are beneficial, especially in the context of life without a gallbladder. The absence of the gallbladder demands significant adjustments in how your body handles dietary fats. Since the gallbladder's primary role is to store and concentrate bile, which helps in the digestion of fat, the direct discharge of bile from the liver to the small intestine post-removal can lead to challenges digesting high-fat meals. Therefore, incorporating low-fat options is not just a preference but a necessity to avoid discomfort and support your digestive health.

Creating low-fat dips and spreads from a blend of vegetables, legumes, and low-fat yogurts can bring both richness and brightness to your meals. Take, for example, the humble chickpea turned into a velvety hummus. By swapping traditional ingredients like tahini and oil for yogurt or even reserved chickpea water, the fat content is considerably lowered while still maintaining that smooth, satisfying texture.

Diversity is key to keeping your diet interesting and palatable. Consider the vibrancy a beetroot hummus could add to your table, not just in color but in nutrients and fiber. Or perhaps a roasted carrot and white bean spread that pairs the sweetness of carrots with the creaminess of beans, providing a tasty way to introduce more vegetables into your diet.

The process of creating these spreads can be as nourishing as consuming them. Picture yourself roasting garlic or bell peppers, the aromas filling your kitchen, then blending them with Greek yogurt for a dip that is both aromatic and gut-friendly. These cooking activities aren't just about feeding yourself; they're about cultivating a relationship with your food, understanding its origins, and appreciating the way it fuels your body.

Moreover, nutritional considerations post-gallbladder surgery extends beyond simply reducing fat. Emphasizing ingredients high in soluble fiber can help manage potential post-surgical diarrhea, a common symptom for many patients. Ingredients like avocados, which are rich in healthy fats and fiber, can be used sparingly in a dip to provide texture and nutrients without overloading your system.

Hydration also plays a critical role in managing your digestion. Dips and spreads containing ingredients like cucumbers, zucchini, or yogurt can contribute to your daily fluid intake, supporting digestion and enhancing the texture and taste of your snacks.

Let's not forget about herbs and spices. Introducing herbs like cilantro, dill, or mint can transform a simple dip into a delightful experience, thrilling your taste buds while also offering anti-inflammatory benefits, which are crucial in your recovery process.

While preparing these dips and spreads, use a mindset of experimentation and moderation. Start with small batches to see how your body reacts to different ingredients. This approach minimizes waste and allows you to adjust recipes to better suit your digestive system and palate.

Sharing these creations can also bring joy and support from family and friends. Food is a universal language of connection, and dishes designed to meet your dietary needs can also be a source of enjoyment and health for your loved ones. Educate them about your new dietary landscape, turning each meal into an opportunity for shared learning and close bonding.

Finally, let's talk about storage and longevity. Many homemade dips and spreads can be stored in the refrigerator in an airtight container for several days, ensuring you have healthy options readily available. By preparing these in batches, you streamline your meal preparation and ensure that you always have something delicious and gentle on your stomach at hand.

In embracing a diet that includes low-fat dips and spreads, you're not only nourishing your body but also rekindling a joy for cooking and eating, despite the challenges posed by life without a gallbladder. Each spread you create is a step toward recovery, each dip a celebration of life's flavors, making the journey as delightful as the destination.

ROASTED RED PEPPER HUMMUS

PREPARATION TIME: 10 min. - **COOKING TIME:** None
MODE OF COOKING: None - **SERVINGS:** 6
INGREDIENTS:
- 1 can chickpeas, drained and rinsed
- 1/2 cup roasted red peppers
- 2 Tbsp tahini
- 2 Tbsp lemon juice
- 1 clove garlic, minced
- 2 Tbsp water
- Salt to taste

PROCEDURE:
1. In a food processor, combine chickpeas, roasted red peppers, tahini, lemon juice, garlic, water, and salt.
2. Blend until smooth, adding more water if needed for desired consistency.
3. Serve with fresh vegetables or pita bread.

TIPS:
1. Garnish with a sprinkle of smoked paprika for extra flavor.
2. Store in the refrigerator for up to one week.

NUTRITIONAL VALUES:
Calories: 120, Fat: 4g, Carbs: 16g, Protein: 4g, Sugar: 2g, Cholesterol: 0mg

SPICY JALAPEÑO HUMMUS

PREPARATION TIME: 10 min. - **COOKING TIME:** None
MODE OF COOKING: None - **SERVINGS:** 6
INGREDIENTS:
- 1 can chickpeas, drained and rinsed
- 1 jalapeño, seeds removed and chopped
- 2 Tbsp tahini
- 2 Tbsp lime juice
- 1 clove garlic, minced
- 2 Tbsp water
- Salt to taste

PROCEDURE:
1. In a food processor, combine chickpeas, jalapeño, tahini, lime juice, garlic, water, and salt.
2. Blend until smooth, adding more water if needed for desired consistency.
3. Serve with fresh vegetables or whole grain crackers.

TIPS:
1. Adjust the amount of jalapeño to control the heat level.
2. Top with a drizzle of olive oil for a richer texture.

NUTRITIONAL VALUES:
Calories: 110, Fat: 3.5g, Carbs: 16g, Protein: 4g, Sugar: 1g, Cholesterol: 0mg

HERBED GREEK YOGURT DIP

PREPARATION TIME: 10 min. - **COOKING TIME:** None
MODE OF COOKING: None - **SERVINGS:** 6
INGREDIENTS:
- 1 cup low-fat Greek yogurt
- 1 Tbsp fresh dill, chopped
- 1 Tbsp fresh parsley, chopped
- 1 clove garlic, minced
- 1 Tbsp lemon juice
- Salt and pepper to taste

PROCEDURE:
1. In a bowl, combine Greek yogurt, dill, parsley, garlic, and lemon juice.
2. Stir until well mixed.
3. Season with salt and pepper to taste.
4. Serve with fresh vegetables or whole grain crackers.

TIPS:
1. Add a pinch of cayenne pepper for a bit of heat.
2. Chill in the refrigerator for an hour to let the flavors meld.

NUTRITIONAL VALUES:
Calories: 50, Fat: 1g, Carbs: 3g, Protein: 8g, Sugar: 2g, Cholesterol: 5mg

CUCUMBER-DILL GREEK YOGURT DIP

PREPARATION TIME: 10 min. - **COOKING TIME:** None
MODE OF COOKING: None - **SERVINGS:** 6
INGREDIENTS:

- 1 cup low-fat Greek yogurt
- 1/2 cucumber, grated
- 1 Tbsp fresh dill, chopped
- 1 clove garlic, minced
- 1 Tbsp apple cider vinegar
- Salt and pepper to taste

PROCEDURE:

1. In a bowl, combine Greek yogurt, grated cucumber, dill, garlic, and apple cider vinegar.
2. Mix until smooth and well combined.
3. Season with salt and pepper to taste.
4. Serve with fresh vegetables or pita chips.

TIPS:

1. Squeeze the grated cucumber to remove excess water for a thicker dip.
2. Garnish with extra dill before serving.

NUTRITIONAL VALUES:
Calories: 45, Fat: 1g, Carbs: 4g, Protein: 7g, Sugar: 2g, Cholesterol: 5mg

CREAMY WHITE BEAN SPREAD

PREPARATION TIME: 10 min - **COOKING TIME:** 0 min
MODE OF COOKING: No-Cook - **SERVINGS:** 6
INGREDIENTS:

- 1 can (15 oz) cannellini beans, drained and rinsed
- 2 Tbsp lemon juice
- 1 Tbsp olive oil
- 1 clove garlic, minced
- 1 tsp fresh rosemary, chopped
- Salt and pepper to taste

DIRECTIONS:

1. In a food processor, combine the cannellini beans, lemon juice, olive oil, and garlic.
2. Blend until smooth and creamy.

3. Add rosemary, salt, and pepper, and pulse until well mixed.
4. Serve immediately or refrigerate for up to 3 days.

TIPS:

1 Serve with fresh vegetables or whole-grain crackers.
2 Add a dash of paprika for a hint of spice.
3 Use as a spread for sandwiches or wraps.

NUTRITIONAL VALUES:
Calories: 110, Fat: 3g, Carbs: 16g, Protein: 4g, Sugar: 0g, Cholesterol: 0mg, Sodium: 140mg

SPICY BLACK BEAN HUMMUS

PREPARATION TIME: 10 min - **COOKING TIME:** 0 min
MODE OF COOKING: No-Cook - **SERVINGS:** 6
INGREDIENTS:

- 1 can (15 oz) black beans, drained and rinsed
- 2 Tbsp lime juice
- 1 Tbsp tahini
- 1 clove garlic, minced
- 1 tsp ground cumin
- 1/2 tsp cayenne pepper
- Salt to taste
- 1/4 cup water (as needed)

DIRECTIONS:

1. In a food processor, combine black beans, lime juice, tahini, garlic, cumin, and cayenne pepper.
2. Blend until smooth, adding water gradually to achieve desired consistency.
3. Season with salt to taste.
4. Serve immediately or store in the refrigerator for up to 3 days.

TIPS:

1 Garnish with chopped cilantro and a drizzle of olive oil.
2 Pair with carrot sticks or cucumber slices for a refreshing snack.
3 Use as a filling for tacos or burritos.

NUTRITIONAL VALUES:
Calories: 120, Fat: 2g, Carbs: 19g, Protein: 5g, Sugar: 0g, Cholesterol: 0mg, Sodium: 150mg

7.3 SWEET TREATS WITHOUT THE GUILT

Indulging in sweet treats after a meal or as a midday pick-me-up is one of life's simple pleasures. For those adapting to a diet post-gallbladder surgery, the quest for desserts that satisfy the sweet tooth without causing digestive discomfort can seem daunting. However, transitioning to a low-fat, gallbladder-friendly diet doesn't mean you have to say goodbye to all things sweet and delightful. The secret lies in choosing the right ingredients and understanding how to use them to transform what might once have been a guilty pleasure into a guilt-free treat.

Imagine biting into a soft, moist cake that uses ripe bananas and applesauce as replacements for the fat-laden butter. Or picture a gelato-like scoop of strawberry sorbet that gets its silkiness from the natural pectin in fruit rather than from heavy cream. These are not just fantasies but are practical, achievable dessert options that can keep your post-surgery life sweet.

The journey of redefining dessert begins with understanding the role of fats in both digestion and traditional dessert preparation. Without a gallbladder, the body's ability to digest and assimilate fats efficiently is compromised, which can lead to discomfort when consuming rich, fatty sweets. Therefore, the challenge is to minimize fat content while maximizing flavor.

Fruits stand out as ideal ingredients. High in natural sugars and flavor, fruits can be used in numerous ways to craft desserts that are both nutritious and indulgent. For instance, fruit salads don't have to be plain; they can be enhanced with a splash of lime and a hint of fresh mint or ginger to elevate the natural flavors. Baking fruits, such as peaches or pears, can intensify their sweetness and create a warm, comforting dessert that requires no added fats.

Sorbets and smoothie bowls offer another excellent way to harness the natural sweetness and creamy textures of fruits without the need for added fats. By freezing and then blending fruits like berries, mangoes, and bananas, you can enjoy an almost ice-cream-like experience. To these, adding ingredients such as chia seeds or flaxseeds not only boosts nutritional content but also helps in creating a fuller, smoother texture.

Rethinking baking methods and ingredients opens up a new world of possibilities. Traditional recipes often call for large quantities of butter and cream, but with a few adjustments, you can create lusciously soft textures and rich flavors without them. Applesauce, for example, can be a wonderful substitute for butter in many recipes, providing moisture and a slight sweetness that reduces the need for additional sugar. Similarly, using yogurt can add creaminess to cakes and muffins, while significantly cutting down fat content.

Moreover, integrating whole grains into your baking can increase fiber content, which is crucial for those lacking a gallbladder, as fiber helps in digestion and regular bowel movements. Whole wheat flour, oatmeal, and almond flour not only add fiber but also contribute nuttiness and depth to the flavor profile of your desserts.

For those times when nothing but chocolate will do, choosing dark chocolate with a high cocoa content (over 70%) can satisfy those cravings without the high sugar and fat content of milk chocolate. Melted dark chocolate can be drizzled over fruits like strawberries or used in small amounts in baking or making granola bars, providing the chocolate fix you desire without overwhelming your digestive system.

Creating lighter versions of traditional desserts requires creativity but it is highly achievable. A parfait, for example, can be constructed with layers of low-fat Greek yogurt, a drizzle of honey, and layers of granola and fruit for a dessert that feels decadent but sits light on the stomach. Similarly, custards and puddings can be made with low-fat milk or almond milk and thickened with cornstarch instead of eggs and cream, providing a creamy texture without the heavy fat content.

What makes these desserts truly enjoyable is not just their flavors but the peace of mind that comes with knowing they are safe and beneficial for your health post-surgery. By wisely selecting ingredients that align with your dietary needs, you not only care for your digestive health but also open the door to an array of delicious, guilt-free pleasures. Remember, the goal of modifying your diet isn't about restricting yourself—it's about reinventing the way you eat to embrace a healthier, more joyful way of living.

Embracing these new methods of dessert preparation can dramatically enhance your post-surgical diet experience. It's about maintaining the joy of eating well—savoring each bite and knowing that each ingredient serves a purpose both for pleasure and for health. Each spoonful of a carefully prepared low-fat sorbet or a bite of a freshly baked fruit suffice becomes a testament to resilience and the ability to adapt and thrive even after significant life changes such as gallbladder removal.

TROPICAL FRUIT SALAD

PREPARATION TIME: 10 min - **COOKING TIME:** 0 min
MODE OF COOKING: No-Cook - **SERVINGS:** 4
INGREDIENTS:

- 1 mango, peeled and diced
- 1 pineapple, peeled and diced
- 1 cup strawberries, hulled and quartered
- Juice of 1 lime

DIRECTIONS:

1. Combine mango, pineapple, and strawberries in a large bowl.

2. Drizzle lime juice over the fruit and toss gently to combine.

3. Serve immediately or chill for 15 minutes for enhanced flavors.

TIPS:

1 Garnish with fresh mint leaves for a burst of color.

2 Add a handful of blueberries for added antioxidants.

3 Serve over a bed of spinach for a refreshing twist.

NUTRITIONAL VALUES:

Calories: 80, Fat: 0.5g, Carbs: 20g, Protein: 1g, Sugar: 16g, Cholesterol: 0mg, Sodium: 2mg

CITRUS BERRY SALAD

PREPARATION TIME: 10 min - **COOKING TIME:** 0 min
MODE OF COOKING: No-Cook - **SERVINGS:** 4
INGREDIENTS:

- 2 oranges, peeled and segmented
- 1 grapefruit, peeled and segmented
- 1 cup raspberries
- 1 Tbsp honey
- 1 tsp poppy seeds

DIRECTIONS:

1. In a large bowl, combine orange segments, grapefruit segments, and raspberries.

2. Drizzle honey over the fruit and sprinkle with poppy seeds.

3. Gently toss to combine and serve immediately.

TIPS:

1 Add a handful of pomegranate seeds for extra crunch.

2 Serve chilled for a refreshing treat on a hot day.

3 Pair with a dollop of low-fat Greek yogurt for added creaminess.

NUTRITIONAL VALUES:

Calories: 70, Fat: 0.2g, Carbs: 17g, Protein: 1g, Sugar: 14g, Cholesterol: 0mg, Sodium: 1mg

MANGO LIME SORBET

PREPARATION TIME: 10 min - **COOKING TIME:** 0 min
MODE OF COOKING: Freezing - **SERVINGS:** 4
INGREDIENTS:

- 2 ripe mangoes, peeled and diced
- 1/4 cup lime juice
- 2 Tbsp honey
- 1/2 cup water

DIRECTIONS:

1. In a blender, combine mangoes, lime juice, honey, and water.

2. Blend until smooth.

3. Pour the mixture into a shallow dish and freeze for 2-3 hours, stirring every 30 minutes until firm.

4. Scoop into bowls and serve.

TIPS:

1 Garnish with lime zest for added flavor.

2 Use agave syrup instead of honey for a vegan option.

3 Serve immediately for the best texture.

NUTRITIONAL VALUES:

Calories: 90, Fat: 0.2g, Carbs: 23g, Protein: 1g, Sugar: 20g, Cholesterol: 0mg, Sodium: 2mg

RASPBERRY LEMON SORBET

PREPARATION TIME: 10 min - **COOKING TIME:** 0 min
MODE OF COOKING: Freezing - **SERVINGS:** 4
INGREDIENTS:

- 2 cups fresh raspberries
- 1/4 cup lemon juice
- 1/4 cup water
- 2 Tbsp honey

DIRECTIONS:

1. In a blender, combine raspberries, lemon juice, water, and honey.

2. Blend until smooth and strain through a fine sieve to remove seeds.

3. Pour the mixture into a shallow dish and freeze for 2-3 hours, stirring every 30 minutes until firm.

4. Scoop into bowls and serve.

TIPS:

1 Add a few mint leaves to the blender for a refreshing twist.

2 Use maple syrup instead of honey for a different flavor profile.

3 Enjoy with a sprinkle of fresh berries on top.

NUTRITIONAL VALUES:

Calories: 80, Fat: 0.3g, Carbs: 19g, Protein: 1g, Sugar: 15g, Cholesterol: 0mg, Sodium: 1mg

BANANA OATMEAL COOKIES

PREPARATION TIME: 10 min - **COOKING TIME:** 15 min
MODE OF COOKING: Baking - **SERVINGS:** 12
INGREDIENTS:

- 2 ripe bananas, mashed
- 1 cup rolled oats
- 1/4 cup raisins
- 1 tsp vanilla extract

DIRECTIONS:

1. Preheat oven to 350°F (175°C).

2. In a bowl, combine mashed bananas, rolled oats, raisins, and vanilla extract.

3. Mix well until ingredients are evenly distributed.

4. Drop spoonsful of the mixture onto a baking sheet lined with parchment paper.

5. Flatten each cookie slightly with the back of the spoon.

6. Bake for 15 minutes or until golden brown.

7. Allow to cool before serving.

TIPS:

1 Add a pinch of cinnamon for extra flavor.

2 Substitute raisins with dark chocolate chips for a sweeter treat.

3 Store in an airtight container to keep them fresh.

NUTRITIONAL VALUES:

Calories: 80, Fat: 0.5g, Carbs: 19g, Protein: 1g, Sugar: 7g, Cholesterol: 0mg, Sodium: 1mg

APPLE CINNAMON MUFFINS

PREPARATION TIME: 15 min - **COOKING TIME:** 20 min
MODE OF COOKING: Baking - **SERVINGS:** 12
INGREDIENTS:

- 1 1/2 cups whole wheat flour
- 1/2 cup rolled oats
- 1 tsp baking powder
- 1 tsp baking soda
- 1 tsp ground cinnamon
- 1/2 tsp salt
- 1 cup unsweetened applesauce
- 1/2 cup honey
- 2 large eggs
- 1/4 cup skim milk

DIRECTIONS:

1. Preheat oven to 375°F (190°C).

2. In a large bowl, combine whole wheat flour, rolled oats, baking powder, baking soda, cinnamon, and salt.

3. In another bowl, mix applesauce, honey, eggs, and skim milk until well blended.

4. Add wet ingredients to dry ingredients and stir until just combined.

5. Pour batter into a muffin tin lined with paper cups, filling each about two-thirds full.

6. Bake for 20 minutes or until a toothpick inserted into the center comes out clean.

7. Cool in the pan for 5 minutes, then transfer to a wire rack to cool completely.

TIPS:

1 Add chopped nuts or dried fruits for additional texture.

2 Use maple syrup instead of honey for a different flavor.

3 Enjoy warm with a dollop of low-fat yogurt.

NUTRITIONAL VALUES:

Calories: 120, Fat: 1g, Carbs: 26g, Protein: 3g, Sugar: 12g, Cholesterol: 25mg, Sodium: 150mg

CHAPTER 8: SMOOTHIES, JUICES, AND BEVERAGES

8.1 DETOXIFYING SMOOTHIES

Navigating through diet adjustments post-gallbladder surgery can feel like a daunting endeavor, but integrating detoxifying smoothies into your routine offers a palatable and invigorating start to realigning your digestive health. Smoothies are more than just meals in a glass—they're a colorful canvas of nutrients tailored to aid your digestive system, especially when you're adapting to life without a gallbladder.

Imagine sipping on a vibrant blend of green kale, spinach, and cucumber, perhaps with a hint of ginger zing. This isn't just a drink—it's a blend formulated for renewal and rejuvenation. The beauty of detoxifying smooth in particular for individuals without a gallbladder lies in their simplicity and nutritional density. They provide crucial nutrients and are generally easy to digest, which takes a load off your liver and compensates for the bile regulation previously managed by your gallbladder.

Detoxifying smoothies impact the body's natural detoxification pathways—systems crucially taxed in those first post-surgery months when your liver is abruptly tasked with direct bile management. Leafy greens, often predominant in detox smoothies, are powerhouse ingredients. They are rich in chlorophyll, which has been heralded in nutritional circles for its potential in toxin cleansing—a benefit not to be understated when your digestive system is already under stress.

Fruits, the other pillars in these smoothies, play a dual role. They add natural sweetness—making the act of nutrition a simple delight rather than a chore—while contributing antioxidants. Berries, especially, burst with vitamins and are known for their inflammation-reducing properties, something essential in managing the occasional digestive discomforts that may arise after your surgery.

Now, let us address a crucial element often overlooked – the base liquid of these smoothies. The selection here impacts not just taste but also your body's response to the smoothie. Clear, non-dairy bases like coconut water or almond milk are excellent options. They keep the smoothie light and are less likely to cause digestive upset compared to dairy, which can be problematic in high volumes for post-gallbladder surgery diets.

Moreover, with your gallbladder gone, your body faces changes in how it processes fats. Herein lies the beauty of tailored smoothie recipes. By opting for avocados—rich in healthy fats and creamy in texture—you afford your body the luxurious feel of a smoothie that supports your nutritional needs without overburdening your system. Avocados can be particularly favorable, providing the creaminess and mouthfeel that one might miss from more traditional, heavier dairy products.

Herbs and spices too find their moment in these concoctions. Take turmeric, for example, with its curcumin component—an anti-inflammatory marvel that supports liver function and digestion. A small sprinkle not only adds a warm, peppery flavor but boosts your drink's health quotient significantly.

When crafting these smoothies, the process can be as therapeutic as consuming them. The act of selecting your ingredients, washing the vibrant greens, peeling the lush fruits, and blending them into a silky elixir can be incredibly grounding—a moment of connection between your body's nutritional needs and the foods that sustain it.

However, it's important to remember that while detox smoothies are beneficial, they are but one part of a diversified diet. They cleanse but do not sustain alone. Including solid foods that are easy on digestion and align with your post-surgery dietary guidelines is essential for balance and overall health.

Here's another layer of consideration—customization based on individual tolerance and stages of recovery. The journey of healing and adapting to a no-gallbladder diet is uniquely personal. What rejuvenates one person may not suit another perfectly. Hence, experimenting with different fruits, vegetables, and bases opens opportunities to discover what works best for your body's new rhythms.

To blend the perfect detoxifying smoothie, listen to your body and consider how each ingredient effects you. Monitoring your body's responses can provide tailored insights into the unique blend of nutrients it needs at varying points in your recovery.

Your new dietary path sans gallbladder need not be a bland or distressing affair. Infused with vivid colors, infused with life-enriching nutrients, and tailored to your personal dietary needs, detoxifying smoothies are like a morning toast to your health—a cheerful, nourishing start to a day that supports your journey towards digestive wellness and overall vitality. Through each sip, embrace this vibrant method of nourishment and let it be a cornerstone of not just a diet, but a thriving, energetic lifestyle without a gallbladder

GREEN DETOX SMOOTHIE WITH SPINACH AND PINEAPPLE

PREPARATION TIME: 10 min. **COOKING TIME:** None
MODE OF COOKING: Blending - **SERVINGS:** 2
INGREDIENTS:
- 1 cup fresh spinach
- 1 cup pineapple chunks
- 1 banana
- 1 cup coconut water

DIRECTIONS:
1. Place all ingredients into a blender.
2. Blend until smooth.
3. Pour into glasses and serve immediately.

TIPS:
1. Use frozen pineapple for a thicker texture.
2. Add a handful of ice cubes for an extra refreshing smoothie.

N.V.: Calories: 150, Fat: 0.5g, Carbs: 38g, Protein: 2g, Sugar: 27g, Cholesterol: 0mg

GREEN DETOX SMOOTHIE WITH KALE AND APPLE

PREPARATION TIME: 10 min. **COOKING TIME:** None
MODE OF COOKING: Blending - **SERVINGS:** 2
INGREDIENTS:
- 1 cup kale leaves, stems removed
- 1 apple, cored and chopped
- 1/2 cucumber, chopped
- 1 cup water

DIRECTIONS:
1. Add kale, apple, cucumber, and water to a blender.
2. Blend until smooth.

3. Pour into glasses and enjoy immediately.
TIPS:
1. Use a high-speed blender for the smoothest texture.
2. Add a squeeze of lemon juice for extra flavor.

N.V.: Calories: 80, Fat: 0.5g, Carbs: 21g, Protein: 2g, Sugar: 14g, Cholesterol: 0mg

BERRY ANTIOXIDANT BLEND WITH BLUEBERRIES AND POMEGRANATE

PREPARATION TIME: 10 min. **COOKING TIME:** None
MODE OF COOKING: Blending - **SERVINGS:** 2
INGREDIENTS:
- 1 cup fresh blueberries
- 1/2 cup pomegranate seeds
- 1 banana
- 1 cup almond milk

DIRECTIONS:
1. Add blueberries, pomegranate seeds, banana, and almond milk to a blender.
2. Blend until smooth.
3. Pour into glasses and serve immediately.

TIPS:
1. Freeze the banana for a creamier texture.
2. Use pomegranate juice if seeds are not available.

N.V.: Calories: 180, Fat: 2g, Carbs: 41g, Protein: 3g, Sugar: 30g, Cholesterol: 0mg

BERRY ANTIOXIDANT BLEND WITH STRAWBERRIES AND BLACKBERRIES

PREPARATION TIME: 10 min. **COOKING TIME:** None
MODE OF COOKING: Blending - **SERVINGS:** 2
INGREDIENTS:
- 1 cup fresh strawberries, hulled
- 1/2 cup blackberries
- 1/2 cup Greek yogurt
- 1 cup water

DIRECTIONS:
1. Combine strawberries, blackberries, Greek yogurt, and water in a blender.
2. Blend until smooth.
3. Pour into glasses and enjoy immediately.

TIPS:
1. Add a few mint leaves for a refreshing twist.

2. Substitute Greek yogurt with a dairy-free option if needed.

N.V.: Calories: 150, Fat: 1g, Carbs: 32g, Protein: 5g, Sugar: 20g, Cholesterol: 0mg

FIBER-RICH SMOOTHIE WITH CHIA SEEDS AND RASPBERRIES

PREPARATION TIME: 10 min. **COOKING TIME:** None
MODE OF COOKING: Blending - **SERVINGS:** 2
INGREDIENTS:
- 1 cup raspberries
- 1 banana
- 1 Tbsp chia seeds
- 1 cup almond milk

DIRECTIONS:
1. Combine raspberries, banana, chia seeds, and almond milk in a blender.
2. Blend until smooth.

3. Pour into glasses and serve immediately.

TIPS:
1. Soak chia seeds in almond milk for 10 minutes before blending for a thicker texture.
2. Add a handful of spinach for extra fiber and nutrients.

N.V.: Calories: 170, Fat: 4g, Carbs: 33g, Protein: 3g, Sugar: 18g, Cholesterol: 0mg

FIBER-RICH SMOOTHIE WITH OATS AND PEAR

PREPARATION TIME: 10 min. **COOKING TIME:** None
MODE OF COOKING: Blending - **SERVINGS:** 2

INGREDIENTS:
- 1 pear, cored and chopped
- 1/2 cup rolled oats
- 1/2 cup Greek yogurt
- 1 cup water

DIRECTIONS:
1. Add pear, rolled oats, Greek yogurt, and water to a blender.
2. Blend until smooth.
3. Pour into glasses and enjoy immediately.

TIPS:
1. Use overnight soaked oats for a smoother texture.
2. Add a dash of cinnamon for extra flavor.

N.V.: Calories: 200, Fat: 3g, Carbs: 40g, Protein: 6g, Sugar: 15g, Cholesterol: 0mg

8.2 REFRESHING JUICES

Imagine waking up to a morning where the glow through your window isn't just sunlight, but a promise of vitality and refreshing energy — all wrapped up in a tall glass of freshly made juice. Juices, especially those crafted from a mix of fruits and vegetables, have long been celebrated for their detoxifying qualities and ability to infuse the body with a rush of healthful benefits. For individuals grappling with the digestive adjustments post-gallbladder surgery, sipping on a juice can be not just rejuvenating but also a crucial part of their nutritional intake.

The art of juicing strikes a wonderful balance between indulgence and health. It simplifies the consumption of a significant amount of nutrients that might otherwise be daunting to ingest, particularly when your body is recalibrating itself to function without a gallbladder. However, the delightful simplicity of juicing belies the careful thought that must go into selecting the right ingredients to maximize benefits while minimizing discomfort.

As we embark on the exploration of refreshing juices, it's important to understand why these vibrant drinks can be such a beneficial addition to your diet. Without a gallbladder, the body's ability to emulsify fats using bile is compromised, necessitating a diet that's not only low in fat but rich in vitamins and minerals which can be seamlessly absorbed. Juices fulfill this requirement beautifully, offering a bounty of vitamins, minerals, antioxidants, and enzymes that are easy on the digestion and quick to assimilate.

The Healing Virtues of Fruit and Vegetable Juices

Fruits and vegetables are inherently packed with water, a crucial element for maintaining hydration which is fundamental for anyone recovering from surgery. But beyond hydration, these natural foods carry phytonutrients that reduce inflammation, enhance immune function, and support the liver in detoxifying the body — a process that's particularly important when your digestion is adjusting to life without a gallbladder.

When crafting juices, choosing a colorful assortment of fruits and vegetables is key. Dark leafy greens such as spinach and kale are celebrated for their rich vitamin content, particularly B vitamins which are essential for energy metabolism. Carrots and beetroots not only add a sweet flavor but are also loaded with beta-carotene and iron, crucial for replenishment and recovery.

However, what truly makes juicing a joy is the ability to experiment with flavors. Citrus fruits like oranges and lemons can add a zesty freshness, enhancing the flavor while supplementing your diet with vitamin C, which aids iron absorption. Apples and pears include a gentle sweetness and additional fiber which is paramount in managing digestive tract health.

Incorporating Herbal Enhancements

Herbs can transform your juice from a delightful beverage to a potent health elixir. Ginger, for example, is a wonderful addition with its anti-inflammatory properties and its ability to ease nausea — a common symptom for those who have recently undergone gallbladder removal. Mint, on the other hand, is not only refreshing but is also beneficial for the stomach, helping to ease digestion and calm upset stomachs.

Balancing Flavors and Health Benefits

While the health benefits of juicing are abundant, it is crucial to maintain a balance. Juices should complement a balanced diet, not replace it. This is particularly important to ensure you receive enough dietary fiber and protein, which juices alone cannot provide. Moreover, it's key to manage the natural sugar content in juices, especially for those closely monitoring their glucose intake.

Practical Tips for Juicing Post-Gallbladder Removal

Juicing should be approached with enthusiasm but also a bit of caution. The absence of the gallbladder requires a mindful reduction of fatty intakes, and while juices are generally low in fat, the incorporation of certain products, like coconut water or avocado, should be moderated. It's ideal to aim for a balance where the majority of your juices focus on vegetables, complemented by a judicious addition of fruits to keep the sugar level in check.

Always listen to your body. If a particular juice combination causes bloating or discomfort, modify your ingredients. Each person's digestive system will react differently post-surgery, and finding what uniquely supports your recovery is key. Starting with simpler juices, perhaps a blend of leafy greens and an apple, can be a gentle way to introduce your digestive system to juiced foods.

In conclusion, embracing a routine of consuming freshly prepared juices can be a delightful and beneficial addition to your recovery diet. Each glass is an opportunity to feed your body with essential nutrients in a form that minimizes digestive stress. Moreover, the act of preparing and consuming these bright, flavorful concoctions is not only a treat for the palate but a boost for the spirit — a cheerful reminder that nourishing your body can be both delicious and rejuvenating.

CITRUS SUNSHINE JUICE

PREPARATION TIME: 10 min. **COOKING TIME:** None **MODE OF COOKING:** Juicing - **SERVINGS:** 2

INGREDIENTS:
- 2 oranges, peeled
- 1 grapefruit, peeled
- 1 lemon, peeled
- 1 tsp honey (optional)

DIRECTIONS:
1. Juice the oranges, grapefruit, and lemon.
2. Stir in honey if desired.
3. Pour into glasses and serve immediately.

TIPS:
1. Chill the fruits beforehand for a cooler juice.
2. Garnish with a mint leaf for a refreshing touch.

N.V.: Calories: 120, Fat: 0g, Carbs: 31g, Protein: 2g, Sugar: 25g, Cholesterol: 0mg

---

WATERMELON MINT JUICE

PREPARATION TIME: 10 min. **COOKING TIME:** None **MODE OF COOKING:** Juicing - **SERVINGS:** 2

INGREDIENTS:
- 3 cups watermelon, cubed
- 1 lime, peeled
- 5 fresh mint leaves

DIRECTIONS:

1. Juice the watermelon and lime.
2. Add mint leaves to the juicer and blend well.
3. Pour into glasses and serve immediately.

TIPS:

1. Serve over ice for an extra refreshing drink.
2. Add a splash of sparkling water for a fizzy twist.

N.V.: Calories: 100, Fat: 0g, Carbs: 26g, Protein: 1g, Sugar: 23g, Cholesterol: 0mg

GREEN GARDEN JUICE

PREPARATION TIME: 10 min. **COOKING TIME:** None **MODE OF COOKING:** Juicing - **SERVINGS:** 2
INGREDIENTS:

- 1 cucumber
- 3 celery stalks
- 1 handful spinach
- 1 green apple

DIRECTIONS:

1. Juice the cucumber, celery, spinach, and green apple.
2. Stir well.
3. Pour into glasses and serve immediately.

TIPS:

1. Add a squeeze of lemon for extra zest.
2. Serve over ice for a refreshing touch.

N.V.: Calories: 70, Fat: 0g, Carbs: 17g, Protein: 2g, Sugar: 10g, Cholesterol: 0mg

CARROT GINGER ZING JUICE

PREPARATION TIME: 10 min. **COOKING TIME:** None **MODE OF COOKING:** Juicing - **SERVINGS:** 2
INGREDIENTS:

- 4 carrots
- 1-inch fresh ginger
- 1 orange, peeled
- 1/2 lemon, peeled

DIRECTIONS:

1. Juice the carrots, ginger, orange, and lemon.
2. Mix well.
3. Pour into glasses and enjoy immediately.

TIPS:

1. Add a pinch of turmeric for an anti-inflammatory boost.

2. Garnish with a carrot stick for a fun presentation.

N.V.: Calories: 90, Fat: 0g, Carbs: 22g, Protein: 1g, Sugar: 18g, Cholesterol: 0mg

CUCUMBER MINT REFRESHER

PREPARATION TIME: 10 min. **COOKING TIME:** None **MODE OF COOKING:** Blending - **SERVINGS:** 2
INGREDIENTS:

- 1 cucumber, peeled and chopped
- 5 fresh mint leaves
- 1 cup coconut water
- 1 tsp honey (optional)

DIRECTIONS:

1. Blend cucumber, mint leaves, coconut water, and honey (if using) until smooth.
2. Strain the mixture through a fine mesh sieve.
3. Pour into glasses and serve chilled.

TIPS:

1. Garnish with a slice of cucumber for added flair.
2. Add a squeeze of lime for a citrus twist.

N.V.: Calories: 45, Fat: 0g, Carbs: 11g, Protein: 1g, Sugar: 6g, Cholesterol: 0mg

WATERMELON BASIL COOLER

PREPARATION TIME: 10 min. **COOKING TIME:** None **MODE OF COOKING:** Blending - **SERVINGS:** 2
INGREDIENTS:

- 3 cups watermelon, cubed
- 5 fresh basil leaves
- 1/2 cup cold water

DIRECTIONS:

1. Blend watermelon, basil leaves, and cold water until smooth.
2. Strain the mixture through a fine mesh sieve.
3. Pour into glasses and serve over ice.

TIPS:

1. Freeze watermelon cubes before blending for a slushier texture.
2. Add a pinch of sea salt to enhance the sweetness.

N.V.: Calories: 60, Fat: 0g, Carbs: 15g, Protein: 1g, Sugar: 12g, Cholesterol: 0mg

Embarking on a new dietary journey after gallbladder surgery can be soothing and even enlightening, especially when we explore the delicately aromatic world of herbal teas and other digestive-friendly beverages. In this cozy corner of our nutritional changes, we find not just comfort but also gentle aids to digestion and well-being.

Imagine a chilly evening or a serene morning where the ritual of tea brewing provides not just a warm cup in hand but a healing touch to your digestive system. Herbal teas, unlike their caffeine-laden counterparts, are not just soothing; they possess qualities that can ease abdominal discomfort, reduce inflammation, and encourage proper digestion—attributes especially beneficial for those sans' gallbladder.

The Therapeutic Embrace of Herbal Teas

Herbal teas are a tapestry of nature's flora—each leaf, flower, and root telling a story of health and healing. For instance, peppermint tea, with its lively aroma, goes beyond its refreshing flavor. It acts as a muscle relaxant, soothing the intestines and easing the spasms that can occur post-meal. Sipping a cup of peppermint tea after dinner isn't just a pleasing ritual; it's a strategic move against post-digestive discomfort.

Then there's chamomile, a mild but mighty flower, often associated with relaxation and sleep. Its benefits extend to digestive health by reducing inflammation and calming upset stomachs. Its gentle nature makes it perfect for evening consumption, setting the stage for a restful night without digestive distress.

Ginger's Warmth: Beyond the Spice

Ginger tea brings warmth and spice, which can kickstart a sluggish digestive system—a common complaint after gallbladder removal. A fresh slice of ginger steeped in boiling water may significantly reduce feelings of nausea and facilitate smoother digestion. It's a piquant remedy, particularly useful when fatty meals might have been more than what your system can comfortably handle.

The Understated Power of Dandelion Root

Often overlooked, dandelion root tea is a powerhouse for liver support. With the gallbladder gone, the liver works overtime in bile production and management. Helping it along with a cup of dandelion tea can enhance its functionality and support your overall digestion. Its earthy tones are grounding, bringing a sense of stability to both mind and body.

Fennel Seeds: A Versatile Digestive Aid

Less a tea than a tisane, fennel seeds can be brewed into a potent drink that offers relief from bloating and gas. Its licorice-like flavor enriches the palette while its digestive enzymes aid the stomach in breaking down food more efficiently.

Harnessing Nature's Hydration: Infused Waters

Stepping beyond the herb garden, another way to embrace digestive wellness is through infused waters. Simple to prepare, these beverages involve steeping fruits, herbs, and even vegetables in water, creating a nutrient-rich hydration source. Cucumber and mint, or lemon and ginger, provide not just flavor but essential hydration that aids in digestion and overall health. After gallbladder surgery, maintaining hydration is crucial as it helps to dilute the bile and facilitate its flow, reducing potential complications and discomfort.

Digestive Harmony with Infused Herbal Waters

Expanding on the theme of infusions, herbal digestive drinks can be created by combining various herbs known for their digestive benefits into a single, powerful drink. A concoction of mint, ginger, and perhaps a hint of turmeric can serve as a daily tonic that not only pleases the taste buds but also supports digestive health.

The Quiet Elegance of Licorice Root

Returning to the warming embrace of teas, licorice root deserves mention. While it is sweet and soothing, it also possesses properties that can alleviate gastrointestinal symptoms such as heartburn and acid reflux, which might be exacerbated post-surgery. However, its use should be moderated as excessive intake can lead to higher blood pressure.

The Healing Touch of Homemade Broths

While not a 'tea' by traditional definitions, the inclusion of homemade broths in our discussion bridges the gap between solid meals and liquid healing. Bone broth, rich in minerals and collagen, can be sipped throughout the day to nurture the body, provide essential nutrients, and ensure that digestion remains as seamless as possible.

GINGER MINT DIGESTIVE TEA

PREPARATION TIME: 5 min. **COOKING TIME:** 10 min. **MODE OF COOKING:** Steeping - **SERVINGS:** 2

INGREDIENTS:
- 1-inch fresh ginger, sliced
- 5 fresh mint leaves
- 2 cups water
- 1 tsp honey (optional)

DIRECTIONS:
1. Bring water to a boil.
2. Add ginger slices and mint leaves to the boiling water.
3. Reduce heat and simmer for 10 minutes.
4. Strain into cups and add honey if desired.

TIPS:
1. Use fresh ginger for the best flavor and benefits.
2. Add a slice of lemon for extra zest and vitamin C.

N.V.: Calories: 10, Fat: 0g, Carbs: 3g, Protein: 0g, Sugar: 1g, Cholesterol: 0mg

CHAMOMILE FENNEL DIGESTIVE TEA

PREPARATION TIME: 5 min. **COOKING TIME:** 5 min. **MODE OF COOKING:** Steeping - **SERVINGS:** 2

INGREDIENTS:
- 2 tsp dried chamomile flowers
- 1 tsp fennel seeds
- 2 cups boiling water

DIRECTIONS:
1. Place chamomile flowers and fennel seeds in a teapot.
2. Pour boiling water over the herbs.
3. Steep for 5 minutes, then strain into cups.
4.

TIPS:
1. Sweeten with a teaspoon of honey if desired.
2. Enjoy before bedtime for a calming effect.

N.V.: Calories: 5, Fat: 0g, Carbs: 1g, Protein: 0g, Sugar: 0g, Cholesterol: 0mg

LEMON CUCUMBER INFUSED WATER

PREPARATION TIME: 5 min. **COOKING TIME:** None **MODE OF COOKING:** Infusing - **SERVINGS:** 4

INGREDIENTS:
- 1 lemon, thinly sliced
- 1/2 cucumber, thinly sliced
- 1 quart (1 liter) water
- A few fresh mint leaves (optional)

DIRECTIONS:
1. Place lemon and cucumber slices into a large pitcher.
2. Add water and mint leaves if using.
3. Refrigerate for at least 2 hours to infuse flavors.
4. Serve chilled.

TIPS:
1. Use filtered water for a cleaner taste.
2. Refill the pitcher with water throughout the day to continue enjoying the flavors.

N.V.: Calories: 5, Fat: 0g, Carbs: 1g, Protein: 0g, Sugar: 0g, Cholesterol: 0mg

STRAWBERRY BASIL INFUSED WATER

PREPARATION TIME: 5 min. **COOKING TIME:** None **MODE OF COOKING:** Infusing - **SERVINGS:** 4

INGREDIENTS:
- 1 cup strawberries, hulled and sliced
- 5 fresh basil leaves
- 1 quart (1 liter) water
-

DIRECTIONS:
1. Place strawberries and basil leaves into a large pitcher.
2. Add water.
3. Refrigerate for at least 2 hours to infuse flavors.
4. Serve chilled.

TIPS:
1. Lightly crush basil leaves to release more flavor.
2. Add ice cubes to keep the water cold for longer.

N.V.: Calories: 10, Fat: 0g, Carbs: 2g, Protein: 0g, Sugar: 1g, Cholesterol: 0mg

TURMERIC GINGER ELIXIR

PREPARATION TIME: 5 min. **COOKING TIME:** 5 min. **MODE OF COOKING:** Boiling - **SERVINGS:** 2

INGREDIENTS:

- 1 tsp turmeric powder
- 1-inch fresh ginger, sliced
- 2 cups water
- 1 tsp honey (optional)
-

DIRECTIONS:

1. Bring water to a boil.
2. Add turmeric powder and ginger slices.
3. Simmer for 5 minutes.
4. Strain into cups and add honey if desired.

TIPS:

1. Add a pinch of black pepper to enhance turmeric absorption.
2. Drink warm for the best anti-inflammatory benefits.

N.V.: Calories: 15, Fat: 0g, Carbs: 4g, Protein: 0g, Sugar: 1g, Cholesterol: 0mg

PINEAPPLE TURMERIC SMOOTHIE

PREPARATION TIME: 5 min. **COOKING TIME:** None **MODE OF COOKING:** Blending - **SERVINGS:** 2

INGREDIENTS:

- 1 cup pineapple chunks
- 1 banana
- 1/2 tsp turmeric powder
- 1 cup coconut water

DIRECTIONS:

1. Add pineapple chunks, banana, turmeric powder, and coconut water to a blender.
2. Blend until smooth.
3. Pour into glasses and serve immediately.

TIPS:

1. Add a small piece of fresh ginger for extra anti-inflammatory properties.
2. Use frozen pineapple for a thicker consistency.

N.V.: Calories: 120, Fat: 0g, Carbs: 31g, Protein: 1g, Sugar: 22g, Cholesterol: 0m

CHAPTER 9: PLANT-BASED RECIPES FOR BETTER DIGESTION

9.1 PROTEIN-PACKED PLANT-BASED MEALS

Navigating the world of plant-based meals can be a delightful exploration, especially after adjusting to the absence of a gallbladder. This exploration invites a plethora of benefits, not just from a health perspective but also in terms of environmental advocacy and ethical dining practices. For those who have undergone gallbladder removal surgery, incorporating protein-packed plant-based meals into one's diet carries a significance that extends beyond basic nutrition. It becomes part of a recuperative journey that enhances digestive well-being and overall health.

When we delve into plant-based eating, the initial concern often revolves around protein. Where do we find adequate protein sources to support bodily functions, especially in a diet devoid of animal products? Plants can indeed provide all the protein necessary for a healthy diet, and discovering this can be both surprising and liberating.

The beauty of plant-based proteins lies in their diversity and the way they encourage creativity in the kitchen. Beans, lentils, chickpeas, tofu, and tempeh stand out as staples. Each of these ingredients carries its own unique profile of not just protein, but also fiber, vitamins, and minerals, which are all crucial for individuals managing their health post-surgery. High in protein and low in fat, these foods help maintain the feeling of fullness without overburdening the digestive system.

Tofu, often dubbed as a blank canvas, soaks up flavors from herbs, spices, and marinades, making it a versatile ingredient in a variety of dishes from stir-fry to grilled plates. Similarly, tempeh, with its firm texture and nutty flavor, can provide an excellent base for dishes that require a hearty component. These soy-based products not only pack a protein punch but also contain isoflavones, which have been linked to improved heart health—a significant consideration for those on a recovery path.

Lentils and chickpeas, meanwhile, are not only rich in protein but are excellent sources of fiber, which helps regulate digestion—a major concern for those without a gallbladder. They can be transformed into warm, soothing stews or vibrant salads that provide both nutrition and satisfaction without straining the digestive system.

However, the transformative journey of adopting a plant-based diet involves more than just substituting meat with plant protein; it's about relearning how to balance meals. For instance, pairing grains like quinoa or brown rice with beans ensures a complete protein profile, akin to that found in meats. This synergy between different plant-based ingredients not only ensures nutritional adequacy but also introduces an array of textures and flavors to the dining table.

Moreover, embracing whole grains is particularly beneficial. Foods like barley, millet, and whole wheat are not only high in fiber but also support a healthy digestive system by providing the necessary bulk to help manage the quicker intestinal transit time experienced by those without a gallbladder.

The psychological and social aspects of shifting towards a plant-based diet post-gallbladder removal are as significant as the physical health benefits. There is often a profound sense of empowerment that comes from taking control of one's diet and health. The decision to go plant-based can also stem from a desire to align more closely with sustainable and ethical eating practices, which resonate with many recovering patients as they reconsider their lifestyles and impact on the world.

Kitchen practices also shift notably. Preparing plant-based meals might mean investing in a good blender for purees and smoothies, a pressure cooker for quick and effective legume preparation, or high-quality knives for efficient vegetable prep. The culinary techniques also pivot towards gentler cooking methods like steaming or sautéing rather than frying, focusing on herbs and spices for flavor rather than heavy sauces or excessive oils.

In the process of embracing plant-based proteins in a diet post-gallbladder removal, there is also a crucial aspect of community and support. Many find encouragement and inspiration through cooking classes, online communities, or local groups that share a focus on plant-based living. This sense of community can provide necessary emotional and motivational support as one navigates their post-surgery dietary adjustments.

The journey toward a plant-based diet rich in proteins and low in fats is not just about meeting dietary requirements—it's a path filled with discoveries, challenges, and victories. It signifies a movement towards not merely surviving without a gallbladder but thriving, using food as both medicine and a source of joy.

Therefore, the emphasis in transitioning to plant-based meals isn't just about replacing lost proteins but about creating a sustainable, flavorful, and nutritious diet that supports both the body and the mind. It's a holistic approach that considers every aspect, from nutritional content and cooking methods to emotional well-being and ecological impact. This comprehensive approach ensures that each meal not only nourishes but also satisfies, making the path to recovery both delicious and joyous.

CRISPY BAKED TOFU WITH HERBS

PREPARATION TIME: 10 min - **COOKING TIME:** 30 min
MODE OF COOKING: Baking - **SERVINGS:** 4
INGREDIENTS:

- 1 lb. firm tofu, pressed and cubed
- 2 Tbsp olive oil
- 1 tsp garlic powder
- 1 tsp dried thyme
- 1 tsp dried basil
- Salt and pepper to taste

PROCEDURE:

1. Preheat oven to 400°F (200°C).
2. In a bowl, toss tofu cubes with olive oil, garlic powder, thyme, basil, salt, and pepper.
3. Spread tofu cubes on a baking sheet lined with parchment paper.
4. Bake for 30 minutes, flipping halfway through, until golden and crispy.
5. Serve warm with a side of steamed vegetables or a fresh salad.

TIPS:

1. Pressing tofu removes excess moisture, making it crispier when baked.
2. Use parchment paper to prevent sticking and make clean-up easier.

NUTRITIONAL VALUES: Calories: 180, Fat: 12g, Carbs: 8g, Protein: 14g, Sugar: 1g, Cholesterol: 0mg

TEMPEH STIR-FRY WITH BROCCOLI

PREPARATION TIME: 10 min - **COOKING TIME:** 15 min
MODE OF COOKING: Stir-frying - **SERVINGS:** 4
INGREDIENTS:

- 1 lb. tempeh, sliced
- 2 Tbsp low-sodium soy sauce
- 1 Tbsp sesame oil
- 1 head broccoli, cut into florets
- 2 cloves garlic, minced
- 1 inch ginger, minced
- 1 Tbsp sesame seeds (optional)

PROCEDURE:

1. Heat sesame oil in a large pan over medium-high heat.
2. Add garlic and ginger, sauté for 1 minute until fragrant.
3. Add tempeh slices, cook for 5 minutes until browned.
4. Add broccoli florets and soy sauce, stir-fry for 5-7 minutes until broccoli is tender.
5. Sprinkle with sesame seeds before serving.

TIPS:

1. Marinate tempeh in soy sauce for 30 minutes before cooking for extra flavor.
2. Serve over brown rice or quinoa for a complete meal.

NUTRITIONAL VALUES: Calories: 220, Fat: 11g, Carbs: 14g, Protein: 19g, Sugar: 2g, Cholesterol: 0mg

HEARTY RED LENTIL STEW

PREPARATION TIME: 10 min - **COOKING TIME:** 25 min
MODE OF COOKING: Simmering - **SERVINGS:** 4
INGREDIENTS:

- 1 cup red lentils, rinsed
- 1 onion, chopped
- 2 cloves garlic, minced
- 1 tsp ground cumin
- 1 tsp ground coriander
- 4 cups vegetable broth

- 1 Tbsp olive oil
- 1 can diced tomatoes (14 oz)

PROCEDURE:
1. Heat olive oil in a large pot over medium heat.
2. Add onion and garlic, sauté until softened, about 5 minutes.
3. Stir in cumin and coriander, cook for 1 minute.
4. Add red lentils, vegetable broth, and diced tomatoes.
5. Bring to a boil, then reduce heat and simmer for 20 minutes, until lentils are tender.
6. Adjust seasoning with salt and pepper to taste. Serve hot.

TIPS:
1. Garnish with fresh cilantro for added flavor.
2. Serve with whole grain bread for a complete meal.

NUTRITIONAL VALUES: Calories: 250, Carbs: 40g, Protein: 12g, Sugar: 5g, Cholesterol: 0mg, Fat: 6g

SPICED GREEN LENTIL AND SPINACH STEW

PREPARATION TIME: 10 min - **COOKING TIME:** 35 min
MODE OF COOKING: Simmering - **SERVINGS:** 4
INGREDIENTS:
- 1 cup green lentils, rinsed
- 1 onion, chopped
- 3 cloves garlic, minced
- 1 tsp ground turmeric
- 1 tsp ground cumin
- 5 cups vegetable broth
- 2 cups fresh spinach, chopped
- 1 Tbsp olive oil

PROCEDURE:
1. Heat olive oil in a large pot over medium heat.
2. Add onion and garlic, sauté until softened, about 5 minutes.
3. Stir in turmeric and cumin, cook for 1 minute.
4. Add green lentils and vegetable broth.
5. Bring to a boil, then reduce heat and simmer for 30 minutes, until lentils are tender.
6. Stir in chopped spinach and cook for an additional 5 minutes.
7. Adjust seasoning with salt and pepper to taste. Serve hot.

TIPS:
1. Add a squeeze of lemon juice before serving for a bright flavor.

2. Top with a dollop of low-fat yogurt for creaminess.

NUTRITIONAL VALUES: Calories: 220, Carbs: 35g, Protein: 15g, Sugar: 3g, Cholesterol: 0mg

MEDITERRANEAN QUINOA BOWL

PREPARATION TIME: 10 min - **COOKING TIME:** 15 min
MODE OF COOKING: Boiling - **SERVINGS:** 4
INGREDIENTS:
- 1 cup quinoa, rinsed
- 2 cups water
- 1 cup cherry tomatoes, halved
- 1 cucumber, diced
- 1/4 cup Kalamata olives, sliced
- 2 Tbsp olive oil
- 1 Tbsp lemon juice
- 1 tsp dried oregano

PROCEDURE:
1. In a medium pot, bring quinoa and water to a boil.
2. Reduce heat to low, cover, and simmer for 15 minutes, until water is absorbed and quinoa is tender.
3. Fluff quinoa with a fork and let cool slightly.
4. In a large bowl, combine cooked quinoa, cherry tomatoes, cucumber, and olives.
5. In a small bowl, whisk together olive oil, lemon juice, and oregano. Pour over quinoa mixture and toss to combine.
6. Season with salt and pepper to taste. Serve at room temperature or chilled.

TIPS:
1. Add crumbled feta cheese for extra flavor.
2. Garnish with fresh parsley or basil.

NUTRITIONAL VALUES: Calories: 210, Carbs: 28g, Protein: 6g, Sugar: 2g, Cholesterol: 0mg, Fat: 9g

SOUTHWESTERN QUINOA BOWL

PREPARATION TIME: 10 min - **COOKING TIME:** 15 min
MODE OF COOKING: Boiling - **SERVINGS:** 4
INGREDIENTS:
- 1 cup quinoa, rinsed
- 2 cups water
- 1 can black beans (15 oz), rinsed and drained
- 1 cup corn kernels (fresh or frozen)
- 1 red bell pepper, diced
- 1 avocado, sliced
- 1/4 cup salsa

- 2 Tbsp lime juice
- 1/2 tsp ground cumin

PROCEDURE:

1. In a medium pot, bring quinoa and water to a boil.
2. Reduce heat to low, cover, and simmer for 15 minutes, until water is absorbed and quinoa is tender.
3. Fluff quinoa with a fork and let cool slightly.
4. In a large bowl, combine cooked quinoa, black beans, corn, and red bell pepper.
5. In a small bowl, mix salsa, lime juice, and cumin. Pour over quinoa mixture and toss to combine.
6. Top with sliced avocado and serve.

TIPS:

1. Add chopped cilantro for added freshness.
2. Serve with a dollop of Greek yogurt for a creamy texture.

NUTRITIONAL VALUES: Calories: 240, Carbs: 35g, Protein: 8g, Sugar: 3g, Cholesterol: 0mg, Fat: 8g

9.2 FIBER-RICH VEGETABLE DISHES

In the journey of adapting to life without a gallbladder, finding meals that are both nutritious and gentle on your digestive system is essential. While the human body can adjust remarkably to the absence of this small organ, the changes in bile flow can make digestion particularly challenging, especially when it comes to fiber-rich foods. However, with the right techniques and understanding, incorporating a range of fiber-rich vegetable dishes can transform your post-surgery diet into one that supports your health and satisfies your palate.

Fiber, crucial for digestive health, can be a double-edged sword in a no-gallbladder diet. On one hand, it helps regulate bowel movements and prevents constipation, a common concern post-surgery. On the other, too much fiber can lead to bloating and discomfort. This is where the magic of balance and preparation comes in, making fiber-rich vegetables not just manageable but beneficial.

Let's embark on a culinary exploration, focusing on vegetables that provide a comfortable amount of fiber suitable for those without a gallbladder. The secret lies in the types of vegetables you choose and how you prepare them. For instance, some vegetables like kale and broccoli can cause bloating when eaten in large quantities or when raw. However, when these are cooked properly, they become more digestible, allowing you to reap their nutritional benefits without discomfort. Roasting vegetables is a wonderful technique to enhance their natural sweetness and make them easier on the stomach. The slow caramelization of the natural sugars in vegetables like carrots, bell peppers, and sweet potatoes not only brings out delightful flavors but also breaks down the fibers, making them less irksome to your digestive system. Imagine the comforting aroma of roasted butternut squash or the satisfying crunch of roasted Brussels sprouts, both offering nourishment in the most delightful way.

Another technique is steaming, which retains nutrients better than many other cooking methods and also softens vegetables to make them gentler on your system. Steamed vegetables maintain more of their original texture and color compared to boiling. Adding herbs like ginger, which is known for its digestive benefits, to steamed vegetables can enhance their flavor and digestive compatibility.

Incorporating soups into your diet is another excellent strategy to include fiber-rich vegetables. Cooking vegetables in a soup softens their fibers significantly, making them easier to digest. A pureed vegetable soup, for example, can be a soothing and nutrient-packed meal. Vegetables like zucchini, squash, and pumpkins blend into a creamy consistency that's both satisfying and gentle on a sensitive digestive tract. Enhancing these soups with herbs like turmeric, which is celebrated for its anti-inflammatory properties, not only adds layers of flavor but also aids in digestion and boosts overall health.

Salads, though generally recommended to be consumed cautiously post-gallbladder removal, can still play a modest part in your dietary regime when prepared thoughtfully. Opt for greens that are easier on the gut, such as butter lettuce or spinach, rather than more fibrous greens like Swiss chard or kale. Incorporating cooked grains such as quinoa or barley can add a soft texture and additional fiber without overwhelming your system. Dress these salads with a simple dressing of lemon juice and a touch of olive oil—a low-fat option that lends flavor without the addition of creams or heavy oils.

Transitioning to a more fibrous diet without a gallbladder is about embracing gradual changes. Start with small portions of fiber-rich foods and observe how your body reacts, slowly adjusting according to your own digestive comfort. This personalized approach ensures that you can enjoy the benefits of a diverse plant-based diet while maintaining digestive comfort.

The narrative of fiber-rich vegetables in a no-gallbladder diet is one of caution and creativity. It's about transforming potential challenges into a testament of your adaptability and commitment to your health. By exploring gentle cooking methods, choosing the right vegetables, and listening to your body's responses, you create not just meals but experiences that support your wellbeing.

Each vegetable dish tells a story of adaptation and resilience—much like your own journey navigating life post-gallbladder removal. These dishes are more than just food; they are companions in your journey towards recovery and health.

ROASTED VEGETABLES

RAINBOW ROASTED VEGETABLE MEDLEY
PREPARATION TIME: 10 min - **COOKING TIME:** 25 min
MODE OF COOKING: Roasting - **SERVINGS:** 4
INGREDIENTS:
- 1 red bell pepper, sliced
- 1 yellow bell pepper, sliced
- 1 zucchini, sliced
- 1 red onion, cut into wedges
- 1 cup cherry tomatoes
- 2 Tbsp olive oil
- 1 tsp dried thyme
- Salt and pepper to taste

PROCEDURE:
1. Preheat oven to 400°F (200°C).
2. In a large bowl, combine all the vegetables.
3. Drizzle with olive oil, sprinkle with thyme, salt, and pepper, and toss to coat.
4. Spread the vegetables in a single layer on a baking sheet.
5. Roast for 25 minutes, stirring halfway through, until vegetables are tender and lightly browned.
6. Serve warm as a side dish or over quinoa for a complete meal.

TIPS:
1. Use a mix of colorful vegetables for visual appeal.
2. Add a splash of balsamic vinegar for added flavor before serving.

NUTRITIONAL VALUES: Calories: 130, Carbs: 15g, Protein: 3g, Sugar: 6g, Cholesterol: 0mg, Fat: 7g

SIMPLE STEAMED BROCCOLI AND SPINACH

PREPARATION TIME: 5 min - **COOKING TIME:** 10 min
MODE OF COOKING: Steaming - **SERVINGS:** 4
INGREDIENTS:
- 1 head broccoli, cut into florets
- 4 cups fresh spinach leaves
- 1 Tbsp olive oil
- 1 lemon, cut into wedges
- Salt and pepper to taste
-

PROCEDURE:
1. Bring a pot of water to a boil and place a steamer basket over it.
2. Add broccoli florets to the steamer basket, cover, and steam for 7 minutes.
3. Add spinach leaves and steam for an additional 3 minutes, until wilted.
4. Transfer steamed greens to a serving dish.
5. Drizzle with olive oil, season with salt and pepper, and serve with lemon wedges.

TIPS:
1. For added flavor, sprinkle with a pinch of garlic powder before steaming.
2. Serve as a side dish or mix into whole grain dishes for a nutritious boost.

NUTRITIONAL VALUES: Calories: 70, Carbs: 7g, Protein: 3g, Sugar: 2g, Cholesterol: 0mg, Fat: 4g

HEARTY VEGETABLE LENTIL SOUP

PREPARATION TIME: 15 min - **COOKING TIME:** 35 min
MODE OF COOKING: Simmering - **SERVINGS:** 4
INGREDIENTS:
- 1 cup green lentils, rinsed
- 1 onion, chopped
- 2 carrots, diced
- 2 celery stalks, diced
- 3 cloves garlic, minced
- 1 can diced tomatoes (14 oz)
- 4 cups vegetable broth
- 1 tsp dried thyme

- 1 tsp cumin
- 2 cups kale, chopped
- 1 Tbsp olive oil

PROCEDURE:

1. Heat olive oil in a large pot over medium heat.
2. Add onion, carrots, and celery; sauté until softened, about 5 minutes.
3. Add garlic and cook for another minute.
4. Stir in lentils, diced tomatoes, vegetable broth, thyme, and cumin.
5. Bring to a boil, then reduce heat and simmer for 25 minutes.
6. Add chopped kale and simmer for an additional 10 minutes, until lentils are tender.
7. Season with salt and pepper to taste. Serve hot.

TIPS:

1. Add a splash of lemon juice before serving for a bright finish.
2. Serve with a slice of whole grain bread for added fiber.

NUTRITIONAL VALUES: Calories: 220, Carbs: 34g, Protein: 11g, Sugar: 6g, Cholesterol: 0mg, Fat: 5g

9.3 VEGAN AND VEGETARIAN DELIGHTS

When embarking on a journey toward recovery and health post-gallbladder surgery, embracing a plant-based diet can seem like venturing into a lush, unexplored garden. Each step through this garden reveals new delights — vibrant tastes and textures that not only promise to soothe your digestive system but also invigorate your entire dining experience. In the realm of vegan and vegetarian cuisine, there is a treasure trove of meals that are not only gentle on the stomach but also deeply nourishing and satisfying.

Picture the humble beginnings of a plant-based meal. You might start with the basics — tofu, tempeh, and an array of colorful vegetables. These are not merely substitutes for meat; they stand proudly as the stars of their own show. Tofu, with its chameleon-like ability to absorb flavors, and tempeh, with its pleasantly nutty bite, offer not just protein but possibilities. They can be grilled, sautéed, or tossed into a spicy curry. Vegetables — the backbone of any vegan or vegetarian diet — bring both color and nutrients to your plate, ensuring that each meal is as pleasing to the eye as it is to the palate.

But why consider this shift, especially after gallbladder surgery? For many, the absence of the gallbladder means that fat digestion can be challenging. Heavy, greasy meals might become foes, causing discomfort or worse. Here, the plant-based realm gently steps in, offering a cornucopia of low-fat options. Think of lentil stews, rich in fiber and protein but naturally low in fat, or roasted vegetables drizzled lightly with olive oil, their natural sugars caramelizing to perfection in the heat of an oven.

The art of seasoning plays a pivotal role in transforming these simple ingredients into extraordinary meals. Herbs and spices do more than just add flavor; they bring their own set of digestive aids. Ginger, turkey, cumin, and coriander, frequently used in plant-based recipes, can help stimulate digestion and reduce inflammation. A sprinkle of these can turn a basic dish into a therapeutic meal.

Perhaps there exists a misconception that plant-based diets are monotonous. Let's dispel this myth by diving into the variety offered by international cuisines. Imagine the zest of a Thai tofu stir-fry, the warmth of an Indian dal, or the comforting embrace of an Italian pasta primavera where zucchini ribbons twirl around your fork in place of spaghetti. Each dish not only satiates your taste buds but also brings you closer to a state of health and equilibrium.

Transitioning to such a diet isn't just about subtracting meat or animal products; it's about re-imagining your plate and your palate. It involves discovering the richness of whole grains like quinoa and barley, which not only provide essential nutrients and fiber but also have a satisfying texture and versatility. Coupled with legumes and seeds, these grains form a robust foundation for any meal, ensuring that you feel full and content.

In crafting meals centered around vegetables, legumes, and grains, there's a gentle thread of creativity that weaves through. You learn to listen to your body, to tweak meals according to what feels nourishing and light. Over time, this listening deepens into an intuitive understanding of your dietary needs, making meal planning not just a necessity but a joyful act of self-care.

Furthermore, embracing a plant-based diet in this new phase of your life might also ripple outwards, influencing your household. Meals can become shared experiences that invite curiosity and foster a sense of wellbeing. They can transform your kitchen from a place of necessity to a space of exploration and connection. Imagine your family gathering over a hearty, aromatic chickpea stew, finding comfort in both the meal and each other's company. Here, food transcends its physical sustenance, becoming a catalyst for healing and togetherness.

Yet, the practicalities of such dietary adjustments might raise concerns, especially when balancing this with a busy lifestyle. Here's where the beauty of batch cooking and meal prep comes into play. A Sunday afternoon spent preparing and freezing portions of lentil soup or veggie burgers can ease your weekly cooking duties. Incorporating plant-based eating into your life doesn't have to be labor-intensive; it can adapt to fit your rhythm, your needs.

Lastly, let's touch upon the emotional layer of dietary changes after surgery. It's natural to feel a sense of loss or frustration as you navigate your new dietary restrictions. However, adopting a plant-based diet can be a creative and empowering response. It's not just about adapting to a new way of eating but about reclaiming control and nurturing your body through thoughtful, nutritious choices.

CHICKPEA AND SPINACH CURRY

PREPARATION TIME: 10 min - **COOKING TIME:** 20 min
MODE OF COOKING: Stovetop - **SERVINGS:** 4
INGREDIENTS:
- 1 can chickpeas, drained and rinsed
- 2 cups fresh spinach
- 1 cup light coconut milk
- 1 Tbsp curry powder

DIRECTIONS:
1. Heat a large skillet over medium heat.
2. Add the chickpeas and curry powder, stirring until chickpeas are well-coated and heated through.
3. Pour in the coconut milk and bring to a gentle simmer.
4. Add the spinach, stirring until wilted and combined.
5. Serve hot.

TIPS:
1. Add a squeeze of lemon juice for extra brightness.
2. Pair with brown rice for a more filling meal.

N.V.: Calories: 180, Carbs: 24g, Protein: 6g, Sugar: 2g, Cholesterol: 0mg, Fat: 6g

QUINOA AND ROASTED VEGETABLE SALAD

PREPARATION TIME: 10 min - **COOKING TIME:** 20 min
MODE OF COOKING: Stovetop and Oven - **SERVINGS:** 4
INGREDIENTS:
- 1 cup quinoa, rinsed
- 2 cups mixed vegetables (e.g., bell peppers, zucchini, cherry tomatoes), chopped
- 1 Tbsp olive oil
- 1 lemon (juice and zest)

DIRECTIONS:
1. Preheat oven to 400°F (200°C).
2. Cook quinoa according to package instructions.
3. Toss vegetables with olive oil and spread on a baking sheet. Roast for 20 minutes until tender.
4. In a large bowl, combine cooked quinoa, roasted vegetables, lemon juice, and zest. Mix well.
5. Serve warm or chilled.

TIPS:
1. Add fresh herbs like parsley or basil for extra flavor.
2. Use seasonal vegetables for variety.

N.V.: Calories: 220, Carbs: 32g, Protein: 6g, Sugar: 4g, Cholesterol: 0mg, Fat: 8g

BROCCOLI AND BELL PEPPER STIR-FRY

PREPARATION TIME: 10 min - **COOKING TIME:** 10 min
MODE OF COOKING: Stovetop - **SERVINGS:** 4
INGREDIENTS:
- 2 cups broccoli florets
- 1 red bell pepper, sliced
- 2 Tbsp low-sodium soy sauce
- 1 Tbsp olive oil

DIRECTIONS:
1. Heat olive oil in a large skillet or wok over medium-high heat.
2. Add broccoli and bell pepper, stir-fry for 5-7 minutes until tender-crisp.
3. Pour in soy sauce, stirring to coat vegetables evenly. Cook for another 2-3 minutes.
4. Serve hot over rice or quinoa.

TIPS:
1. Add a pinch of red pepper flakes for a spicy kick.
2. Top with sesame seeds for added texture.

N.V.: Calories: 80, Carbs: 10g, Protein: 3g, Sugar: 2g, Cholesterol: 0mg, Fat: 4g

CHAPTER 10: INTERNATIONAL FLAVORS FOR A DIVERSE DIET

10.1 MEDITERRANEAN CUISINE

Embarking on a culinary journey through the Mediterranean after gallbladder surgery can be both a delightful exploration and a gentle way to reintroduce your body to the world of diverse flavors without overwhelming your digestive system. The essence of Mediterranean cuisine lies in its reliance on fresh, whole ingredients, minimal use of heavy, fatty cooking techniques, and an abundant use of herbs and spices, making it an ideal choice for those adapting to life without a gallbladder.

Imagine walking through a bustling Mediterranean market. The air is filled with the enticing aromas of fresh herbs, citrus, and the unmistakable freshness of just-caught fish. This scene isn't just picturesque; it's indicative of a dietary richness that supports gentle digestion while being abundantly flavorful. At the heart of Mediterranean cooking is the use of olive oil, an excellent source of monounsaturated fat, which is easier on your digestion compared to the saturated fats found in butter and certain cuts of meat.

The transformative power of olive oil extends beyond its health benefits; it carries the flavors of spices and herbs, infusing dishes with nuances that are both delicate and robust. For someone managing their diet post-gallbladder surgery, olive oil provides a necessary fat component that aids in the absorption of vitamins without taxing your system.

As we delve deeper into the Mediterranean palette, let's talk about the region's hallmark: its diversity of fresh produce. Vegetables play a starring role in dishes like Greek salads or ratatouille, a French dish that celebrates the simplicity of stewed vegetables. The key here is the slow cooking process, which melds the flavors beautifully and makes each bite easy to digest. Incorporating these vegetable-centric dishes into your diet ensures you are not only savoring the flavors of the region but also receiving ample fiber, which is crucial for your digestive health post-surgery.

Seafood, too, forms an integral part of Mediterranean cuisine. Grilled or baked fish, seasoned simply with herbs, lemon, and a drizzle of olive oil, provides high-quality protein and omega-3 fatty acids that are essential for inflammation reduction, which can be a concern post-surgery. The simplicity of Mediterranean seafood preparations ensures that your meals are both nourishing and lightweight, avoiding the heaviness that typically accompanies richer, cream-based dishes or heavily marinated meats.

The beauty of Mediterranean cuisine also lies in its herbs and spices, like basil, oregano, rosemary, and thyme. These aren't just flavor enhancers; they have inherent digestive benefits. For instance, rosemary has been known for its anti-inflammatory properties, while basil can help ease gas and soothe stomach discomfort, common complaints in the post-surgery period.

Continuing with our market tour, imagine now the delicate aroma of fresh herbs mingling with the robust presence of garlic and onions. While these ingredients are staples in Mediterranean cooking, they may initially seem daunting if you've experienced digestion issues post-gallbladder removal. However, cooking them sufficiently until soft and fragrant can mitigate adverse effects, allowing you to enjoy their health benefits and taste without discomfort.

Let's not overlook the role of legumes in this cuisine. Foods like lentils, chickpeas, and beans are used extensively in Mediterranean recipes, from Moroccan chickpea stews to Greek lentil soups. These ingredients are not only hearty and satisfying but also provide a substantial amount of dietary fiber that aids in smooth digestion. It's essential, though, to introduce them slowly and in moderation into your diet to assess how your body adjusts without the gallbladder.

Moreover, the tradition of enjoying meals slowly, savoring each bite, is woven into the fabric of Mediterranean dining culture. This practice is particularly beneficial for those without a gallbladder, as taking your time with meals can significantly improve digestion and reduce symptoms like bloating and discomfort.

As you adapt these culinary practices and dishes to your new dietary needs, the focus should always remain on balancing flavors with what is best for your body. The Mediterranean approach offers not just recipes but a lifestyle that embraces healthy fats, plenty of produce, and the joys of eating meals that are both socially and nutritionally fulfilling.

Incorporating Mediterranean cuisine into your post-gallbladder removal diet isn't just about managing your digestive health; it's about expanding your palate and enjoying your meals to the fullest without feeling restricted. As you explore these new flavors and dishes, remember that each ingredient and technique can be tailored to meet your specific nutritional needs, ensuring every meal is not only a treat for your taste buds but also a step towards recovery and long-term well-being. This culinary adventure, rooted in tradition and health, is not just about adapting to a new way of eating—it's about thriving through it.

CLASSIC GREEK SALAD

PREPARATION TIME: 10 min - **COOKING TIME:** 0 min
MODE OF COOKING: Raw - **SERVINGS:** 4
INGREDIENTS:
- 2 cups cherry tomatoes, halved
- 1 cucumber, diced
- 1/2 red onion, thinly sliced
- 1/2 cup Kalamata olives
- 1/4 cup feta cheese, crumbled
- 2 Tbsp extra-virgin olive oil
- 1 Tbsp red wine vinegar
- 1 tsp dried oregano
- Salt and pepper to taste

DIRECTIONS:
1. In a large bowl, combine cherry tomatoes, cucumber, red onion, and olives.
2. Sprinkle crumbled feta cheese over the vegetables.
3. In a small bowl, whisk together olive oil, red wine vinegar, oregano, salt, and pepper.
4. Pour the dressing over the salad and toss gently to combine.
5. Serve immediately.

TIPS:
1. Add fresh mint or parsley for extra flavor.
2. Serve with whole grain pita bread for a complete meal.

N.V.: Calories: 150, Carbs: 10g, Protein: 3g, Sugar: 4g, Cholesterol: 10mg, Fat: 12g

OLIVE OIL AND LEMON ROASTED POTATOES

PREPARATION TIME: 10 min - **COOKING TIME:** 30 min
MODE OF COOKING: Roasting - **SERVINGS:** 4
INGREDIENTS:
- 4 medium potatoes, peeled and cut into wedges
- 3 Tbsp extra-virgin olive oil
- Juice of 1 lemon
- 1 tsp dried oregano
- Salt and pepper to taste

DIRECTIONS:
1. Preheat oven to 400°F (200°C).
2. In a large bowl, combine potato wedges, olive oil, lemon juice, oregano, salt, and pepper. Toss to coat evenly.
3. Spread the potatoes in a single layer on a baking sheet.
4. Roast in the oven for 30 minutes or until golden brown and crispy, turning halfway through.
5. Serve hot.

TIPS:
1. Add garlic cloves to the roasting pan for extra flavor.
2. Garnish with fresh parsley before serving.

N.V.: Calories: 180, Carbs: 30g, Protein: 3g, Sugar: 2g, Cholesterol: 0mg, Fat: 7g

LOW-FAT TZATZIKI

PREPARATION TIME: 10 min - **COOKING TIME:** 0 min
MODE OF COOKING: Raw - **SERVINGS:** 4
INGREDIENTS:
- 1 cup Greek yogurt (low-fat)
- 1 cucumber, grated and drained
- 2 cloves garlic, minced
- 1 Tbsp lemon juice
- 1 Tbsp fresh dill, chopped
- Salt and pepper to taste

DIRECTIONS:

1. In a medium bowl, combine Greek yogurt, grated cucumber, minced garlic, lemon juice, and chopped dill.
2. Mix well until all ingredients are fully incorporated.
3. Season with salt and pepper to taste.
4. Chill in the refrigerator for at least 30 minutes before serving to allow flavors to meld.

TIPS:

1. Serve with whole grain pita chips or fresh vegetable sticks.
2. Add a splash of olive oil on top for extra richness.
3. Use as a healthy sandwich spread.

N.V.: Calories: 60, Carbs: 4g, Protein: 5g, Sugar: 3g, Cholesterol: 5mg, Fat: 2g

10.2 ASIAN-INSPIRED DISHES

Embarking on a culinary journey through Asia can offer a delightful array of flavors that are not just tantalizing to the taste buds but can also be wonderfully accommodating for those who are adapting to a life without a gallbladder. The rich tapestry of Asian cuisine provides a treasure trove of dishes that emphasize fresh ingredients, gentle cooking methods, and a harmonious balance of nutrients, making it an excellent choice for anyone mindful of digestive health.

In many Asian cultures, food is a celebration of community and health—a philosophy that aligns well with the essentials of post-gallbladder diet management. Consider the subtlety and diversity of Asian cooking styles: from the steamy bowls of Vietnamese pho to the stir-fried vegetables of a Chinese meal, each dish offers unique insights into how to prepare meals that are both nourishing and easy to digest.

The cornerstone of integrating Asian-inspired dishes into a gallbladder-free diet is the use of techniques like steaming, poaching, and quick stir-frying. Such methods not only preserve the integrity and nutritional value of the ingredients but also ensure that meals are lighter and less taxing on your digestive system. Imagine steaming a delicate fillet of fish with ginger—its flavor both soothing and invigorative—or tossing a crisp array of vegetables in a hot wok for a quick stir-fry, using just a touch of heart-friendly oil like canola or sesame.

The ingredients typical in Asian cuisines also lend themselves well to a low-fat diet. Tofu, a staple in many Asian kitchens, serves as a perfect source of plant-based protein, and its versatile nature means it can be seamlessly included in a variety of dishes, from Japanese miso soups to Indonesian tofu curries. Similarly, the liberal use of vibrant herbs and spices—like turmeric, which is known for its anti-inflammatory properties, or ginger, celebrated for its gastrointestinal benefits—adds depth and complexity to dishes without the need for excessive fats or oils.

Navigating the rich world of Asian grains offers yet another venue for culinary exploration. Brown rice and buckwheat noodles provide excellent fiber-rich alternatives to traditional white rice or noodles, which are often more challenging to digest post-surgery. These grains not only complement the textures and flavors of Asian dishes but also contribute to a feeling of fullness and digestive ease.

Let's also embrace the use of mushrooms, a revered ingredient across many Asian cuisines. Varieties like shiitake, maitake, and enoki are not only celebrated for their umami-rich profiles but are also known for their health-promoting properties, including boosting immune function and supporting heart health. Used in broths, stir-fries, or as a meat substitute, mushrooms can elevate a simple meal into something truly special while being gentle on the stomach.

Another aspect of Asian culinary culture that resonates with a post-gallbladder diet is the tradition of small, frequent meals. This practice aligns beautifully with the need to manage portion sizes to aid digestion. A traditional Korean meal with its banchan (small side dishes), for example, allows one to enjoy a varied array of nutrients and tastes in modest, digestible amounts. This encourages eating at a slower pace, which is crucial for those managing their digestion post-surgery, allowing the body to better process smaller quantities of fats and other hard-to-digest nutrients.

Furthermore, the Asian tradition of ending the meal with tea can also be particularly beneficial. Green tea, for instance, with its antioxidant properties and ability to aid digestion can be a soothing conclusion to any meal. In a similar vein, fresh herbal brews like ginger tea can act as digestives, helping to settle the stomach and reduce bloating.

While the flavors and techniques of Asian cuisine offer numerous benefits for those without a gallbladder, it's also worth mentioning how to manage the use of certain ingredients that may be challenging. Traditional dishes that involve deep-fried elements or use coconut milk, which is high in saturated fats, should be adapted. Opting for light stir-frying or substituting with low-fat coconut milk alternatives can ensure you still enjoy the richness of Asian flavors without compromising your dietary needs.

In practice, adapting Asian dishes to fit a gallbladder-free lifestyle is about making thoughtful substitutions, not about foregoing flavor. By replacing heavier ingredients with lighter ones, and by incorporating plenty of vegetables, lean proteins, and beneficial herbs and spices, one can create a meal that is not only safe and comforting but also exciting and culturally enriching.

Embracing the light, aromatic, and nutritious components of Asian cuisine can significantly enrich your diet post-gallbladder removal. Not only are these dishes delightful on the palate and gentle on the stomach, but they also bring the added joy of exploring new culinary landscapes—turning each meal into a small celebration of recovery and health

GINGER GARLIC STIR-FRIED VEGETABLES

PREPARATION TIME: 10 min - **COOKING TIME:** 10 min
MODE OF COOKING: Stovetop - **SERVINGS:** 4
INGREDIENTS:

- 2 cups mixed vegetables (e.g., bell peppers, broccoli, snap peas)
- 1 Tbsp olive oil
- 2 cloves garlic, minced
- 1-inch piece of ginger, grated
- 2 Tbsp low-sodium soy sauce

DIRECTIONS:

1. Heat olive oil in a large skillet or wok over medium-high heat.
2. Add minced garlic and grated ginger, stir-fry for 1-2 minutes until fragrant.
3. Add mixed vegetables and stir-fry for 5-7 minutes until tender-crisp.
4. Pour in soy sauce and stir to coat vegetables evenly. Cook for another 2 minutes.
5. Serve hot over brown rice or quinoa.

TIPS:

1. Add a splash of sesame oil for extra flavor.
2. Top with toasted sesame seeds for added texture.
3. Use a mix of colorful vegetables for visual appeal and nutritional variety.

N.V.: Calories: 90, Carbs: 10g, Protein: 3g, Sugar: 2g, Cholesterol: 0mg, Fat: 4g

TERIYAKI TOFU RICE BOWL

PREPARATION TIME: 10 min - **COOKING TIME:** 15 min
MODE OF COOKING: Stovetop - **SERVINGS:** 4
INGREDIENTS:

- 1 cup brown rice, cooked
- 1 block firm tofu, cubed
- 2 cups mixed vegetables (e.g., broccoli, carrots, bell peppers)
- 1/4 cup teriyaki sauce

DIRECTIONS:

1. Cook brown rice according to package instructions.
2. In a large skillet, heat a small amount of oil over medium heat. Add cubed tofu and cook until golden brown on all sides, about 5-7 minutes.
3. Add mixed vegetables to the skillet and stir-fry for 5 minutes until tender.
4. Pour teriyaki sauce over tofu and vegetables, stirring to coat evenly. Cook for an additional 2-3 minutes.
5. Serve the tofu and vegetable mixture over a bed of brown rice.

TIPS:

1. Garnish with sesame seeds for added texture.
2. Add sliced green onions for a fresh flavor.
3. Use low-sodium teriyaki sauce for a healthier option.

N.V.: Calories: 320, Carbs: 45g, Protein: 12g, Sugar: 5g, Cholesterol: 0mg, Fat: 8g

LOW-FAT TERIYAKI SAUCE

PREPARATION TIME: 5 min - **COOKING TIME:** 10 min
MODE OF COOKING: Simmering - **SERVINGS:** 8
INGREDIENTS:

- 1/2 cup low-sodium soy sauce
- 1/4 cup water
- 2 Tbsp honey
- 2 tsp rice vinegar
- 1 tsp ginger, minced
- 1 garlic clove, minced
- 1 Tbsp cornstarch mixed with 2 Tbsp water (slurry)

DIRECTIONS:

1. In a small saucepan, combine soy sauce, water, honey, rice vinegar, ginger, and garlic.
2. Bring to a gentle simmer over medium heat, stirring occasionally.
3. Add the cornstarch slurry and stir continuously until the sauce thickens, about 2-3 minutes.
4. Remove from heat and let cool before using or storing.

TIPS:

1. Add a pinch of red pepper flakes for a spicy kick.
2. Use as a marinade or a stir-fry sauce for vegetables and lean proteins.
3. Store in an airtight container in the refrigerator for up to one week.

N.V.: Calories: 20, Carbs: 5g, Protein: 1g, Sugar: 3g, Cholesterol: 0mg, Fat: 0g

10.3 LATIN AMERICAN FLAVORS

Embracing the vibrant and diverse culinary heritage of Latin America offers a delightful journey, especially when navigating a low-fat, gallbladder-friendly diet. The good news is, Latin American cuisine, with its emphasis on fresh ingredients and bold flavors, can be a perfect ally in your post-surgery dietary adaptation.

Picture this: the zest of lime juice, the fragrance of cilantro, and the robust presence of beans and corn. These staple ingredients not only infuse dishes with vibrant flavors but are also conducive to gentle digestion and nutritional balance. The key lies in selecting ingredients and cooking methods that align with your new dietary needs without sacrificing the joy of eating.

Think of the traditional Latin American kitchen—minimal use of heavy creams and rich sauces, with a focus instead on salsas, rubs, and marinades that bring dishes to life. It's not just about making food easier on the stomach; it's about celebrating culture in each bite.

Fresh Salsa and Guacamole: A Festival of Flavors

Salsa and guacamole, the quintessential favorites at any Latin American table, are perfect for those without a gallbladder. Why? Because they are rich in enzymes that aid digestion. Fresh salsa, made from ripe tomatoes, onions, cilantro, and just a splash of lime, can be a refreshing topping for grilled chicken or fish—both excellent protein sources that are easy on a sensitive system.

On the other hand, guacamole, primarily consisting of avocado, provides a wealth of healthy fats. Despite the common misconception, not all fats are your enemy post-gallbladder removal. Avocado contains monounsaturated fat, which is easier for your body to handle and essential for maintaining good heart health. The key is moderation, ensuring that even healthy fats are consumed in a way that respects your liver's new workflow.

Embracing Legumes: The Heart of Comfort

Beans play a pivotal role in Latin American diets. They're not only a hearty, comforting base for many dishes but also provide a solid source of protein and fiber, which are crucial in managing your digestive health. The versatility of legumes allows them to be incorporated into a variety of dishes—from simple black bean soups clear of heavy oils and creams to lentil stews spiced with cummin and a bay leaf for added depth and flavor.

The art is in the preparation. Soaking beans and cooking them thoroughly can help make them more digestive, ultimately preventing the bloating and gas often associated with higher fiber ingredients. Combining them with spices like turmeric, known for its anti-inflammatory properties, can further enhance their digestibility and add an exotic flavor twist that enriches the dining experience.

Reimagining Tortillas and Tacos

The humble corn tortilla, a staple in Latin American kitchens, takes on new life for those who must manage their fat intake carefully. Opt for corn tortillas over flour ones to enjoy a gluten-free, fiber-rich option that is much lighter on your system. Stuff these tortillas with a mix of grilled vegetables, lean meats, or even fish, topped with a dollop of your fresh salsa for a satisfying meal that doesn't skimp on flavor or texture.

Transforming the classics into low-fat alternatives doesn't have to mean losing out on cultural authenticity or taste. Take tacos, for instance—consider making fish tacos using grilled or baked fish instead of fried, seasoned liberally with herbs and spices that compensate for any reduced fat content.

FRESH TOMATO SALSA

PREPARATION TIME: 10 min - **COOKING TIME:** None
MODE OF COOKING: Fresh - **SERVINGS:** 4
INGREDIENTS:

- 4 ripe tomatoes, diced
- 1/2 red onion, finely chopped
- 1 jalapeño, seeded and minced
- 1/4 cup fresh cilantro, chopped
- Juice of 1 lime
- Salt to taste

DIRECTIONS:

1. Combine tomatoes, red onion, jalapeño, and cilantro in a bowl.
2. Add lime juice and salt.
3. Mix well and let sit for 10 minutes to allow flavors to meld.
4. Serve immediately or refrigerate for later use.

TIPS:

1. For a smoky flavor, roast the tomatoes and jalapeño before chopping.
2. Adjust the amount of jalapeño to control the heat level.
3. Use as a topping for grilled meats or as a dip with tortilla chips.

N.V.: Calories: 20, Carbs: 4g, Protein: 1g, Sugar: 2g, Cholesterol: 0mg, Fat: 0g

BLACK BEAN TACOS

PREPARATION TIME: 5 min - **COOKING TIME:** 10 min **MODE OF COOKING:** Sautéing - **SERVINGS:** 4

INGREDIENTS:

- 1 can black beans, rinsed and drained
- 1 avocado, sliced
- 8 small corn tortillas
- 1/4 cup fresh cilantro, chopped

PROCEDURE:

1. Heat a skillet over medium heat and add the black beans. Cook for 5 minutes until heated through.
2. Warm the tortillas in a separate skillet or microwave.
3. Divide the black beans among the tortillas.
4. Top each taco with avocado slices and a sprinkle of cilantro.
5. Serve immediately.

TIPS:

1. Add a squeeze of lime for extra flavor.
2. Sprinkle with a pinch of salt to enhance taste.

NUTRITIONAL VALUES: Calories: 140, Carbs: 20g, Protein: 5g, Sugar: 1g, Cholesterol: 0mg, Fat: 5g

SPINACH AND MUSHROOM TORTILLAS

PREPARATION TIME: 10 min - **COOKING TIME:** 10 min **MODE OF COOKING:** Sautéing - **SERVINGS:** 4
INGREDIENTS:

- 8 small whole wheat tortillas
- 1 cup fresh spinach, chopped
- 1 cup mushrooms, sliced
- 1/4 cup reduced-fat shredded cheese

PROCEDURE:

1. Heat a non-stick skillet over medium heat.
2. Sauté mushrooms until tender, about 5 minutes. Add spinach and cook until wilted, about 2 minutes.
3. Warm tortillas in a separate skillet or microwave.
4. Divide the spinach and mushroom mixture among the tortillas.
5. Sprinkle each tortilla with cheese.
6. Fold tortillas in half and serve immediately.

TIPS:

1. Add a sprinkle of fresh cilantro for extra flavor.
2. Serve with a side of salsa for a spicy kick.

NUTRITIONAL VALUES: Calories: 150, Carbs: 22g, Protein: 7g, Sugar: 2g, Cholesterol: 5mg, Fat: 4g

CHAPTER 11: SOUPS AND BROTHS FOR HEALING

11.1 HEALING BONE BROTHS

Healing begins at the stove, where warmth meets nourishment in the gentle bubbles of a simmering pot. Bone broth, an ancient concourse revered by generations for its restorative properties, plays a pivotal role in the recovery journey for those who've bid farewell to their gallbladder. The beauty of bone broth lies not just in its simplicity, but in the profound way it supports digestion and nurtures the body from within.

Imagine the bones, those sturdy foundations of our very anatomy, releasing their hidden treasures into hot water—minerals, amino acids, collagen—all seeping into the surrounding liquid, creating a broth that's both mild on a sensitive gut and rich in healing nutrients. For anyone adjusting to life after gallbladder surgery, a soothing cup of bone broth can feel like a quiet conversation with an old friend, both comforting and immensely healing.

Creating a bone broth starts with selecting the right bones. Whether from chicken, beef, or fish, these remnants of meals past carry the deep flavors and essential compounds necessary for fostering health. You might picture a busy kitchen where pots clang gently and steam dances up towards a sunny window. Here, the bones are first given new life through roasting, which deepens their flavors, coaxing out rich, caramelized hues that promise a more robust broth.

As these beautifully browned bones meet hot water, their robust character slowly melds into a pool of subtle, nurturing warmth. Onions, carrots, and celery typically join the chorus, contributing their sweet melodies. These vegetables are more than mere flavor enhancers—they bring with them vitamins and fiber, contributing to the broth's nutritional profile without overwhelming the system.

Now, the gentle heat does its ancient work. Simmering, a slow and deliberate process, is where patience meets science. Too vigorous a boil, and the broth becomes cloudy with disrupted proteins and fats—harsh on a system still tender from surgery. Instead, a gentle simmer, barely a whisper of movement beneath the surface, allows for the extraction of nutrients without the violence of a rolling boil.

The simmering pot whispers of transformation, the bones and vegetables slowly giving themselves over to the water. Hour's pass—six, perhaps twelve—as flavors deepen, meld, and become something entirely new. Over time, fat rises to the top, forming a layer that can be skimmed off to ensure that the broth remains as digestible as possible for those lacking a gallbladder's bile storage. This aspect is crucial because post-surgery, the body's ability to emulsify fats is diminished. The long simmer, the careful skimming—these steps ensure a broth that's not only flavorful but also light and nurturing.

But what exactly makes bone broth such a potent healer? The key lies in its components. Collagen, transformed through heat into gelatin, supports gut health and soothes the intestinal lining, making digestion an easier task. The amino acids, like glycine and proline, are the unsung heroes, supporting detoxification and tissue repair—critical processes during recovery. Minerals leach from the bones into the broth, offering easily absorbable forms of calcium, magnesium, phosphorus, and trace elements, fortifying the body without demanding much from the digestive system.

As the broth nears completion, imagine the kitchen filled with its warm, inviting aroma. Straining is the final act of refinement, removing solid bits to leave a clear, nourishing liquid that's as gentle on the stomach as it is satisfying to the soul. This broth can be sipped straight, seasoned lightly with salt and perhaps a squeeze of lemon for brightness. Alternatively, it serves as a base for other dishes, imparted with healing qualities and subtle, enveloping warmth.

For those nursing a body back to health without the gallbladder, incorporating bone broth into the daily diet can be transformative. It's not only about what this humble broth brings nutritionally but also how it soothes, comforts, and nutrifies during a time of adjustment and healing.

In this way, bone broth isn't just food; it's a companion on the journey to wellness, a simple concoction that reaches back through generations, offering the wisdom of the ages in every savory, healing sip. It stands as a testament to the power of simple ingredients and time-honored cooking techniques in fostering health and well-being, especially when the body is navigating the complexities of health post-surgery.

CLASSIC BONE BROTH

PREPARATION TIME: 10 min - **COOKING TIME:** 10 hrs **MODE OF COOKING:** Simmering - **SERVINGS:** 8

INGREDIENTS:

- 2 lb. beef bones
- 2 carrots, chopped
- 2 celery stalks, chopped
- 1 onion, quartered
- 2 Tbsp apple cider vinegar
- 10 cups water
- Salt to taste

PROCEDURE:

1. Preheat oven to 400°F (200°C). Roast bones for 30 minutes.
2. Transfer bones to a large pot. Add carrots, celery, onion, and vinegar.
3. Pour in water and bring to a boil. Reduce to a simmer.
4. Simmer for 10 hours, skimming foam occasionally.
5. Strain the broth through a fine-mesh sieve. Season with salt.

TIPS:

1. For richer flavor, roast the vegetables with the bones.
2. Store in the fridge for up to 5 days or freeze for later use.

NUTRITIONAL VALUES: Calories: 50, Carbs: 2g, Protein: 6g, Sugar: 1g, Cholesterol: 0mg, Fat: 1g

VEGETABLE-ENHANCED BONE BROTH

PREPARATION TIME: 15 min - **COOKING TIME:** 10 hrs **MODE OF COOKING:** Simmering - **SERVINGS:** 8

INGREDIENTS:

- 2 lb. beef bones
- 2 carrots, chopped
- 2 celery stalks, chopped
- 1 onion, quartered
- 1 leek, chopped
- 1 zucchini, chopped
- 1 tomato, halved
- 2 Tbsp apple cider vinegar
- 10 cups water
- Salt and pepper to taste
- 2 bay leaves
- 1 bunch parsley

PROCEDURE:

1. Preheat oven to 400°F (200°C). Roast bones for 30 minutes.
2. Transfer bones to a large pot. Add carrots, celery, onion, leek, zucchini, tomato, and vinegar.
3. Pour in water and bring to a boil. Reduce to a simmer.
4. Add bay leaves and parsley. Simmer for 10 hours, skimming foam occasionally.
5. Strain the broth through a fine-mesh sieve. Season with salt and pepper.

TIPS:

1. Use a slow cooker to make this process even easier.
2. Add a splash of lemon juice for extra brightness before serving.

NUTRITIONAL VALUES: Calories: 60, Carbs: 4g, Protein: 7g, Sugar: 2g, Cholesterol: 0mg, Fat: 1g

CHICKEN AND VEGETABLE RISOTTO

PREPARATION TIME: 10 min - **COOKING TIME:** 30 min **MODE OF COOKING:** Simmering - **SERVINGS:** 4

INGREDIENTS:

- 1 cup Arborio rice
- 4 cups bone broth
- 1 chicken breast, diced
- 1 cup mixed vegetables (peas, carrots, zucchini)
- 1 onion, finely chopped
- 2 cloves garlic, minced
- 1/4 cup grated Parmesan cheese (optional)
- 2 Tbsp olive oil
- Salt and pepper to taste

PROCEDURE:

1. In a large saucepan, heat olive oil over medium heat. Sauté onion and garlic until translucent.
2. Add diced chicken and cook until browned.
3. Stir in Arborio rice and cook for 2 minutes.
4. Gradually add bone broth, one cup at a time, stirring continuously until absorbed.
5. Add mixed vegetables and cook until the rice is creamy and tender, about 20 minutes.
6. Stir in Parmesan cheese (if using) and season with salt and pepper.

TIPS:

1. Use warm bone broth for better absorption.
2. Add a splash of white wine for extra depth of flavor before adding the broth.

NUTRITIONAL VALUES: Calories: 320, Carbs: 40g, Protein: 25g, Sugar: 3g, Cholesterol: 45mg, Fat: 8g

11.2 CREAMY VEGETABLE SOUPS (WITHOUT THE CREAM)

Imagine the comfort of warming up with a bowl of creamy vegetable soup, its rich texture hugging your taste buds, yet without the heaviness—or post-meal discomfort—that can come from traditional cream-based soups. For those of us without a gallbladder, finding ways to enjoy such deeply satisfying meals without compromising on taste or digestive comfort is paramount.

The beauty of vegetable soups lies in their versatility; they're a canvas for culinary creativity and a vessel for nutrition. And though cream is often seen as a requisite for the luxurious texture we crave in a good soup, there are several delightful ways to achieve that heartiness without it. This chapter is dedicated to exploring how to make creamy vegetable soups that are enriching, nourishing, and completely devoid of actual cream, meeting your post-gallbladder removal dietary needs with aplomb.

The Foundation of Creaminess Without Cream

The trick to achieving a creamy consistency in your vegetable soups without the use of actual dairy or high-fat components lies in the choice of ingredients and cooking techniques. Vegetables like cauliflower, potatoes, butternut squash, and carrots are not only packed with nutrients but also have a naturally creamy quality when cooked and blended. Let's look at how these vegetables serve as the perfect base for your cream less soup endeavors.

Cauliflower, for example, is a marvel in the soup-making world. It has a subtle flavor and when cooked and pureed, adds a silken texture to dishes that mimic the richness of cream. Potatoes, albeit high in carbohydrates, contain starches that lend a natural thickness to soups. Butternut squash and carrots, with their slightly sweet profiles, add depth and round out the flavors, presenting a comforting and satisfying bowl of soup.

Cooking Techniques That Enhance Natural Creaminess

The method by which you cook your vegetables can dramatically affect the texture and flavor of your soup. Roasting is one such technique that intensifies the inherent sweetness and richness of vegetables. By roasting butternut squash or carrots before adding them to your soup, you unlock more complex flavors and a deeper sweetness that enhances the natural creaminess of the soup.

Another innovative approach is slow-cooking. This involves letting your vegetables simmer gently, allowing them to break down over time, releasing their flavors and melding together into a cohesive, smooth, and creamy mixture after being puréed.

The Role of Pureeing and the Right Equipment

Once your vegetables are cooked through and tender, the next step is pureeing. This is where the creamy magic happens. A high-quality blender or an immersion blender can be your best friend in achieving a smooth, velvety texture that rivals any cream-laden soup. It's important to blend at a high speed until the mixture is completely smooth; the finer the purée, the creamier the soup.

For those looking to enhance the creaminess further, adding a touch of plant-based milk or a scoop of cooked white beans before blending can enrich the texture. These not only supplement the creaminess but also boost the protein content of your soup, making it more satisfying.

Flavor Enhancements and Their Digestive Impacts

Choosing the right herbs and spices can transform your soup from simple to spectacular, adding layers of flavor that complement the natural taste of the vegetables. Fresh or dried herbs such as thyme, rosemary, and sage offer a comforting aroma and taste that infuse beautifully into vegetable soups.

For a more exotic take, spices like cumin, coriander, and a dash of nutmeg add warmth and complexity. However, it's crucial to gauge how well you tolerate certain spices post-gallbladder surgery, as everyone's digestive system reacts differently. The key is to start with small amounts and adjust according to your body's response.

Integrating Nutritional Considerations

Without the gallbladder playing a role in fat digestion, it becomes more challenging to process high-fat foods, which is why these cream-free vegetable soups are so beneficial. They provide the heartiness and satisfaction of traditional creamy soups but are much easier on your digestive system. Furthermore, by focusing on vegetables, you're ensuring an intake of essential vitamins and antioxidants, which play a crucial role in your overall health and recovery post-surgery.

CREAMY CARROT AND GINGER SOUP

PREPARATION TIME: 10 min - **COOKING TIME:** 25 min **MODE OF COOKING:** Simmering - **SERVINGS:** 4
INGREDIENTS:
- 1 lb. carrots, peeled and chopped
- 1 onion, chopped
- 2 cloves garlic, minced
- 1 Tbsp fresh ginger, grated
- 4 cups vegetable broth
- 2 Tbsp olive oil
- Salt and pepper to taste

PROCEDURE:
1. In a large pot, heat olive oil over medium heat. Sauté onion, garlic, and ginger until fragrant, about 5 minutes.
2. Add carrots and vegetable broth. Bring to a boil, then reduce heat and simmer for 20 minutes, until carrots are tender.
3. Using an immersion blender, blend soup until smooth.
4. Season with salt and pepper to taste.

TIPS:
1. Add a splash of coconut milk for extra creaminess.
2. Garnish with fresh parsley or cilantro before serving.

NUTRITIONAL VALUES: Calories: 130, Carbs: 20g, Protein: 2g, Sugar: 7g, Cholesterol: 0mg, Fat: 5g

CREAMY CAULIFLOWER SOUP

PREPARATION TIME: 10 min - **COOKING TIME:** 25 min **MODE OF COOKING:** Simmering - **SERVINGS:** 4
INGREDIENTS:
- 1 head cauliflower, chopped
- 1 onion, chopped
- 2 cloves garlic, minced
- 4 cups vegetable broth
- 1 cup unsweetened almond milk
- 2 Tbsp olive oil
- Salt and pepper to taste

PROCEDURE:
1. In a large pot, heat olive oil over medium heat. Sauté onion and garlic until translucent, about 5 minutes.
2. Add cauliflower and vegetable broth. Bring to a boil, then reduce heat and simmer for 20 minutes, until cauliflower is tender.
3. Using an immersion blender, blend soup until smooth.
4. Stir in almond milk and season with salt and pepper.

TIPS:
1. Add a pinch of nutmeg for a warm, earthy flavor.
2. Garnish with fresh chives or parsley for added freshness.

NUTRITIONAL VALUES: Calories: 100, Carbs: 10g, Protein: 3g, Sugar: 3g, Cholesterol: 0mg, Fat: 5g

LEEK AND POTATO SOUP WITH HERB INFUSION

PREPARATION TIME: 10 min - **COOKING TIME:** 25 min **MODE OF COOKING:** Simmering - **SERVINGS:** 4
INGREDIENTS:
- 2 leeks, white and light green parts only, sliced
- 2 potatoes, peeled and diced
- 4 cups vegetable broth
- 1 bay leaf
- 2 sprigs thyme
- 1 Tbsp olive oil
- Salt and pepper to taste

PROCEDURE:
1. In a large pot, heat olive oil over medium heat. Sauté leeks until softened, about 5 minutes.
2. Add potatoes, vegetable broth, bay leaf, and thyme. Bring to a boil, then reduce heat and simmer for 20 minutes, until potatoes are tender.
3. Remove bay leaf and thyme sprigs. Using an immersion blender, blend soup until smooth.
4. Season with salt and pepper to taste.

TIPS:
1. Add a swirl of olive oil before serving for extra richness.
2. Garnish with chopped chives or parsley for a fresh finish.

NUTRITIONAL VALUES: Calories: 150, Carbs: 28g, Protein: 3g, Sugar: 3g, Cholesterol: 0mg, Fat: 4g

11.3 LIGHT AND NOURISHING BROTHS

Life after gallbladder removal can often seem overwhelming, especially when it comes to adjusting one's diet to fit this new reality. It isn't just about avoiding discomfort but also about nurturing the body back to health with gentle, soothing meals. Light and nourishing broths are a cornerstone of such a diet, providing essential nutrients without straining the digestive system.

Broths, especially those made from clear vegetables or lean meats like chicken or fish, are more than just comforting—they are a powerful tool in the post-surgery dietary toolkit. These simple concoctions are packed with vitamins and minerals, offering hydration and aiding in the recovery and maintenance of digestive health. Let's explore why these broths are beneficial and how they serve not only as a base for cooking but also as a standalone, soothing drink.

The magic of broths lies in their simplicity and the depth of flavor they can offer while being inherently gentle on the stomach. For those who have undergone gallbladder surgery, the body requires foods that are easy to digest. Foods that are high in fat or hard to break down can cause discomfort or even pain, making recovery more difficult. This is where broths come in—an easily absorbable form of nourishment that contributes to healing without overwhelming the digestive system.

Preparing a basic broth involves simmering meat or vegetables in water, often with herbs and a modest amount of salt to taste. The simmering process allows the flavors to meld and the nutrients to infuse into the water, creating a liquid that is rich in flavor yet light in consistency. Bone broth, made from simmering bones for an extended period, is particularly rich in nutrients like gelatin and collagen, which are known for their health benefits, including supporting joint health and improving gut integrity.

Vegetable broths are equally vital in a no-gallbladder diet. They are not only lower in fat but can be customized according to what your body tolerates best post-surgery. Carrots, celery, and herbs like parsley offer detoxifying properties and provide a comforting flavor base. Adding ginger can enhance the anti-inflammatory properties, while garlic boosts immunity—a perfect blend for someone focusing on recovery.

But perhaps the most therapeutic aspect of broths, particularly for those adjusting to life without a gallbladder, is their role in daily meals. Broth can be sipped alone, used as a cooking liquid for grains like rice or quinoa, or serve as the foundation for more substantial soups and stews. This versatility makes it an indispensable part of the recovery diet, providing variety and nutrition without complication.

Moreover, knowing how to season and enhance broths can transform them from mere nutritional staples into culinary delights. Simple seasonings like thyme, rosemary, and bay leaves can elevate the flavor profile without adding irritants that might upset a sensitive stomach. For a touch of richness, a splash of lemon juice or a sprinkle of finely chopped fresh herbs added towards the end of cooking can brighten the flavors without adding fat.

For those with no gallbladder, every meal and what it contains matter significantly in terms of how the body reacts and processes these meals. A light broth maintains hydration, crucial for aiding digestion and overall health recovery—issues like bloating and indigestion often exacerbated in their absence can be mitigated through regular consumption of these mild liquids.

While it's essential to follow specific dietary guidelines post-gallbladder removal, broths offer a foundation upon which a balanced and fulfilling diet can be built. They couple ease of digestion with the pleasure of nourishment—a combination critical in any recovery process but especially so in one that so fundamentally alters how food is processed by the body.

As we consider the importance of broths in a post-gallbladder removal diet, it's also vital to think about the emotional and psychological elements of eating. Food is not just sustenance; it's a pleasure, a part of social interactions, and often, a source of comfort. Broths are comforting not only in their warmth and simplicity but also in their ability to provide a safe, healing meal at a time when many other foods are off-limits.

Incorporating broths into your diet is a strategy that offers both nutritional and psychological benefits, supporting physical recovery with each spoonful while ensuring that the journey back to health does not feel like a path of constant denial. By understanding the properties of various ingredients and how they work together to support digestive health, broths can be both medicinal and nourishing, stabilizing the diet in ways few other foods can.

Living without a gallbladder indeed presents its unique challenges, but it also encourages a reconnection with food's basic, nourishing elements. Broths represent this reconnection; a return to the fundamentals of nutrition, providing a delicate balance of nutrients necessary for recovery and daily wellbeing without overwhelming the digestive system.

LIGHT VEGETABLE BROTH

PREPARATION TIME: 10 min - **COOKING TIME:** 1 hr **MODE OF COOKING:** Simmering - **SERVINGS:** 6

INGREDIENTS:
- 2 carrots, chopped
- 2 celery stalks, chopped
- 1 onion, quartered
- 2 cloves garlic, smashed
- 1 zucchini, chopped
- 1 bay leaf
- 4 sprigs parsley
- 8 cups water
- Salt to taste

PROCEDURE:
1. In a large pot, combine carrots, celery, onion, garlic, zucchini, bay leaf, and parsley.
2. Add water and bring to a boil. Reduce heat and simmer for 1 hour.
3. Strain the broth through a fine-mesh sieve, discarding solids.
4. Season with salt to taste.

TIPS:
1. Add a splash of soy sauce for an umami boost.
2. Use as a base for soups or stews for added depth of flavor.

NUTRITIONAL VALUES: Calories: 20, Carbs: 4g, Protein: 1g, Sugar: 2g, Cholesterol: 0mg, Fat: 0g

CHICKEN AND FISH BROTHS

SIMPLE CHICKEN BROTH
PREPARATION TIME: 10 min - **COOKING TIME:** 1 hr 30 min
MODE OF COOKING: Simmering - **SERVINGS:** 6
INGREDIENTS:
- 1 lb (450g) chicken bones (preferably with some meat)
- 1 onion, quartered
- 2 carrots, roughly chopped
- 2 celery stalks, roughly chopped
- 3 garlic cloves, smashed
- 1 bay leaf

- 8 cups (2 qt/1.9L) water
- Salt and pepper to taste
-

DIRECTIONS:
1. In a large pot, combine all ingredients.
2. Bring to a boil, then reduce heat to low and simmer for 1.5 hours.
3. Strain the broth through a fine mesh sieve.
4. Season with salt and pepper to taste.

TIPS:
1. Skim off any foam that forms on the surface for a clearer broth.
2. Use the broth as a base for soups or sauces.

N.V.: Calories: 45, Carbs: 5g, Protein: 4g, Sugar: 2g, Cholesterol: 5mg, Fat: 1g

SIMPLE SEASONING IDEAS

SIMPLE SEASONING IDEAS
LEMON HERB SEASONING
PREPARATION TIME: 5 min
COOKING TIME: 0 min
MODE OF COOKING: No cooking - **SERVINGS:** 8
INGREDIENTS:
- 1 lemon, zested
- 1 Tbsp dried thyme
- 1 Tbsp dried rosemary
- 1 tsp garlic powder
- 1 tsp onion powder
- 1/2 tsp salt
- 1/4 tsp black pepper

DIRECTIONS:
1. Combine all ingredients in a small bowl.
2. Mix well and store in an airtight container.
3. Use 1-2 tsp per serving of broth.

TIPS:
1. For a fresher taste, add lemon zest just before serving.
2. This blend pairs well with both chicken and vegetable broths.

N.V.: Calories: 2, Carbs: 0.5g, Protein: 0g, Sugar: 0g, Cholesterol: 0mg, Fat: 0g

CHAPTER 12: DESSERTS AND SWEETS

12.1 LOW-FAT DESSERTS

Navigating the realm of desserts can often feel daunting, especially when you're focused on maintaining a low-fat diet conducive to a life without a gallbladder. The journey to enjoying sweet treats post-surgery might seem peppered with restrictions; however, it's also an opportunity to rediscover the joy in creating and savoring desserts that are both delectable and forgiving on your digestive process.

One of the fundamental shifts when adapting to a low-fat diet is the redefinition of what dessert can look like. Traditionally, desserts are seen as indulgent, often rich in fats and heavy creams. However, focusing on low-fat alternatives doesn't mean sacrificing the sense of satisfaction that a good dessert can bring. This convergence of health and pleasure is not just possible; it's wonderfully achievable.

Embracing Fruit as a Natural Sweetener

Fruits are nature's candy, and their versatility can be a revelation. Think about the rustic charm of a warm, baked apple, spiced with cinnamon and perhaps a touch of honey. Apples are low in fat and the baking process intensifies their natural sweetness, making them a perfect dessert option. Similarly, incorporating a medley of roasted fruits — like peaches, pears, and plums — can create a dessert that is both satisfying and light. Roasting fruits not only caramelizes their natural sugars but also creates a complexity of flavor that can rival any traditional dessert.

Rediscovering Yogurt: A Creamy, Low-Fat Base

Greek yogurt is a stellar substitute for cream in many recipes, offering a creamy texture and a tangy flavor that complements fruits and other natural sweeteners well. By starting with a base of low-fat Greek yogurt, you can add layers of flavors using spices like nutmeg or cardamom, or by mixing in vanilla or almond extract. For a bit of crunch and additional nutrients, a sprinkle of toasted nuts or granola can elevate a simple bowl of yogurt into a dessert that satisfies the craving for something substantial yet healthful.

The Role of Texture and Flavor Enhancements

Texture plays a crucial role in how we enjoy food, and this is particularly true for low-fat desserts. A mousse, for example, traditionally relies on heavy cream for its airy texture. However, by using pureed silken tofu as a base, blended with high-quality cocoa powder and sweetened with agave or stevia, it's possible to achieve a similarly luscious texture that feels indulgent without the heaviness of cream. This not only keeps the fat content low but also adds protein, making it a balanced option for a post-meal treat.

Similarly, flavor enhancements through spices and extracts can turn a simple dish into a symphony of tastes. A dash of cinnamon can add warmth, a sprinkle of citrus zest can bring brightness, and a drizzle of a flavored balsamic vinegar can introduce an unexpected but delightful tang to fruit-based desserts.

The Art of Healthy Substitutions in Baking

For many, baking is a comforting activity, filled with the nostalgia of family recipes and holiday gatherings. Adapting these recipes to fit a low-fat diet can be a joyful challenge that doesn't have to compromise on flavor. For instance, substituting apple sauce or mashed bananas for butter not only reduces the fat content but also adds moisture and a subtle sweetness, excellent for muffins and cakes. Whole grain flours can replace refined ones to increase the nutrient profile, and experimenting with reducing the sugar content can often lead to discovering new flavors and textures in old favorites.

Savoring Each Bite: Mindful Eating and Dessert

Finally, it's essential to cultivate a practice of mindful eating, especially when it comes to enjoying desserts. Desserts are often eaten quickly, perhaps almost guiltily. However, by taking the time to savor each bite, noticing the textures, the layers of flavor, and the pleasure they bring, not only enhances the eating experience but also aligns with the principles of eating well for digestion.

In conclusion, desserts in a low-fat dietary lifestyle post-gallbladder surgery are far from being just about restriction. They are an exploration of flavors, textures, and ingredients that nourish the body and delight the senses. They require us to be creative, thoughtful, and open to new possibilities. Each spoonful of a well-crafted low-fat dessert is not just good for the digestive system; it is a reaffirmation of the joy and abundance that life offers, even within dietary limits. Embrace this journey with excitement, and let each dessert be a celebration of health and flavor.

FRUIT-BASED DESSERTS

HONEY-GLAZED PEACHES
PREPARATION TIME: 10 min - **COOKING TIME:** 15 min
MODE OF COOKING: Grilling - **SERVINGS:** 4
INGREDIENTS:

- 4 ripe peaches, halved and pitted
- 2 Tbsp honey
- 1 tsp ground cinnamon

DIRECTIONS:

1. Preheat grill to medium-high heat.
2. Brush peach halves with honey.
3. Sprinkle with cinnamon.
4. Grill peaches cut-side down for 4-5 minutes, until tender and caramelized.
5. Serve warm.

TIPS:

1. Pair with a dollop of low-fat Greek yogurt.
2. Substitute honey with maple syrup for a different flavor profile.

N.V.: Calories: 80, Carbs: 20g, Protein: 1g, Sugar: 18g, Cholesterol: 0mg, Fat: 0g

APPLESAUCE BROWNIES

PREPARATION TIME: 10 min - **COOKING TIME:** 25 min
MODE OF COOKING: Baking - **SERVINGS:** 12
INGREDIENTS:

- 1 cup unsweetened applesauce
- 1/2 cup cocoa powder
- 1 cup whole wheat flour
- 1/2 cup sugar
- 1 tsp baking powder
- 1/2 tsp salt
- 1 tsp vanilla extract

DIRECTIONS:

1. Preheat oven to 350°F (175°C).
2. In a large bowl, mix applesauce, cocoa powder, sugar, and vanilla extract.
3. Add flour, baking powder, and salt, stirring until just combined.
4. Pour batter into a greased 8x8-inch baking pan.
5. Bake for 25 minutes or until a toothpick inserted in the center comes out clean.
6. Allow to cool before cutting into squares.

TIPS:

1. Add a handful of chopped nuts for extra texture.
2. Serve with a dollop of low-fat Greek yogurt.

N.V.: Calories: 90, Carbs: 21g, Protein: 2g, Sugar: 12g, Cholesterol: 0mg, Fat: 0.5g

YOGURT-BASED TREATS

BERRY YOGURT PARFAIT
PREPARATION TIME: 10 min - **COOKING TIME:** 0 min
MODE OF COOKING: No cooking - **SERVINGS:** 4
INGREDIENTS:

- 2 cups non-fat Greek yogurt
- 1 cup mixed berries (strawberries, blueberries, raspberries)
- 1/4 cup honey
- 1/2 cup granola

DIRECTIONS:

1. In each serving glass, layer 1/2 cup Greek yogurt.
2. Add a layer of mixed berries.
3. Drizzle with 1 Tbsp honey.
4. Top with 2 Tbsp granola.
5. Repeat layers if desired and serve immediately.

TIPS:

1. Use seasonal fruits for the best flavor.
2. Add a sprinkle of chia seeds for extra nutrition.

N.V.: Calories: 150, Carbs: 25g, Protein: 10g, Sugar: 18g, Cholesterol: 0mg, Fat: 1g

When embarking on a journey through a post-gallbladder removal diet, one of the sweetest stops you can make is in the realm of fruit-based treats. After all, fruits are nature's candy, packed with a bounty of vitamins, minerals, and fibers that not only cater to the taste buds but also support digestive health, which is paramount when adapting to changes post-surgery.

Incorporating fruit into your diet is particularly beneficial, as they're generally low in fats and high in the type of fiber that aids slow digestion and helps regulate blood sugar levels, an essential aspect for anyone focusing on gentle dietary changes. However, learning to choose the right fruits and preparing them in ways that maintain their nutritional integrity while making them palatable and satisfying can be both an art and a science.

Imagine savoring a perfectly ripened peach, its juices bursting with every bite, or the crispness of an apple that fills the air with its fresh aroma. These simple pleasures can still be part of your daily routine. In fact, moving towards a lifestyle that includes making fruit-based treats can bring a sense of normalcy and delight post-gallbladder surgery. But it's not just about indulging in fruit as it is; it's about transforming these nutritional powerhouses into dishes that soothe the stomach and please the palate.

The beauty of fruits lies in their versatility. They can be enjoyed raw, cooked, or blended, allowing you to create an array of dishes that can meet your nutritional needs and satisfy your cravings. For instance, baking fruits can unleash new flavors and textures, making them more appealing while being easy on the digestion. Consider a baked apple or pear, subtly sweetened with a hint of cinnamon and perhaps a drizzle of honey—this method enhances the fruit's natural sweetness without the need for much added sugar and makes a delicious, comforting treat that aligns well with your dietary needs.

Moreover, fruits are not just for desserts. They can complement many dishes as side items or even main components. For example, a fresh fruit salad incorporating a variety of colors and textures not only provides visual appeal but also ensures a good intake of different nutrients. Ingredients like oranges, strawberries, and kiwis mixed with some mint leaves can create a refreshing side that stimulates digestion and boosts immune function.

However, it is crucial to be mindful of the types of fruit you select. Some fruits, particularly those that are very high in natural sugars like mangoes or grapes, might need to be enjoyed in moderation to avoid digestive discomfort. Balancer is key. Incorporating fruits with lower glycemic indexes and higher fiber content such as berries and apples can be more beneficial.

In addition, the method of incorporating these fruits into your diet should be considered. Smoothies and juices, for example, can be wonderful ways to consume a concentrated amount of nutrients in an easily digestible form. However, juicing removes the fiber, which is essential for those without a gallbladder to help slow the absorption of sugars and ease digestion. Smoothies, on the other hand, retain all parts of the fruit, making them a better option for a fiber-rich, nutritious snack or meal.

Consider also the innovation of using fruits in gelatins or puddings made with agar-agar or pectin, both of which provide a smooth texture that's easy on the stomach and can help in creating appealing and digestive-friendly desserts. These gelling agents not only enhance the texture but can soothe the digestive tract.

The transition to making fruits a central part of your post-surgery diet also opens the door to exploring diverse cuisines and cultural practices that might rely more heavily on fruits in their cooking. For instance, Middle Eastern cuisine often uses dates and dried apricots in savory dishes, providing sweetness and texture alongside meats and grains. Experimenting with such combinations can reignite a passion for cooking and eating, even within dietary restrictions.

As we explore these fruity avenues, it's also worth noting the importance of organic and pesticide-free options. As someone adapting to life without a gallbladder, it's beneficial to reduce the intake of potential toxins and chemicals that can strain your digestive system. Opting for organic fruits can minimize this risk and enhance the health benefits of your meals.

So, while the journey might seem daunting at first, integrating fruit-based treats into your diet is not just about adhering to restrictions; it's about rediscovering joy in eating and turning nourishment into an act of self-care. With each sweet and tangy bite, you are not just eating; you are healing, celebrating the bounty that nature offers, and taking steps towards a healthier, happier you. This approach to diet after gallbladder surgery isn't just a necessity—it's an opportunity to transform and enrich your culinary world, ensuring each meal not only supports your physical health but also brings a smile to your face

FRESH FRUIT SALADS

FRESH FRUIT SALADS
TROPICAL FRUIT SALAD
PREPARATION TIME: 10 min - **COOKING TIME:** 0 min
MODE OF COOKING: No cooking - **SERVINGS:** 4
INGREDIENTS:

- 1 mango, peeled and diced
- 1 cup pineapple chunks
- 2 kiwis, peeled and sliced
- 1 banana, sliced
- Juice of 1 lime

DIRECTIONS:

1. In a large bowl, combine mango, pineapple, kiwi, and banana.
2. Drizzle with lime juice.
3. Toss gently to combine.
4. Serve immediately.

TIPS:

1. Add a handful of shredded coconut for extra tropical flavor.
2. Chill the fruit before mixing for a refreshing treat.

N.V.: Calories: 90, Carbs: 23g, Protein: 1g, Sugar: 19g, Cholesterol: 0mg, Fat: 0.5g

BAKED FRUITS

BAKED CINNAMON APPLES
PREPARATION TIME: 10 min - **COOKING TIME:** 25 min
MODE OF COOKING: Baking - **SERVINGS:** 4
INGREDIENTS:

- 4 apples, cored
- 2 Tbsp honey
- 1 tsp ground cinnamon
- 1/4 cup raisins (optional)

DIRECTIONS:

1. Preheat oven to 375°F (190°C).
2. Place apples in a baking dish.
3. Drizzle honey over apples and sprinkle with cinnamon.
4. Stuff each apple with a few raisins, if using.
5. Bake for 25 minutes or until apples are tender.
6. Serve warm.

TIPS:

1. Use a mix of apple varieties for added flavor.
2. Serve with a dollop of non-fat Greek yogurt.

N.V.: Calories: 120, Carbs: 32g, Protein: 0.5g, Sugar: 25g, Cholesterol: 0mg, Fat: 0g

TROPICAL MANGO SMOOTHIE BOWL

PREPARATION TIME: 10 min - **COOKING TIME:** 0 min
MODE OF COOKING: Blending - **SERVINGS:** 2
INGREDIENTS:

- 1 ripe mango, peeled and chopped
- 1 banana, frozen
- 1 cup coconut water
- 1/2 cup Greek yogurt (low-fat)

DIRECTIONS:

1. In a blender, combine the mango, banana, coconut water, and Greek yogurt.
2. Blend until smooth and creamy.
3. Pour the mixture into two bowls.

TIPS:

1. Top with fresh berries, chia seeds, and sliced almonds for added texture and nutrients.
2. For a thicker consistency, add more frozen banana or reduce the coconut water.
3. Enjoy immediately for the best flavor and texture.

NUTRITIONAL VALUES: Calories: 200, Carbs: 45g, Protein: 5g, Sugar: 35g, Cholesterol: 5mg, Fat: 1g

12.3 BAKING WITHOUT BUTTER AND CREAM

In the cozy warmth of a kitchen filled with the aroma of freshly baked goods, there's often a sense of comfort and nostalgia. However, for those who've undergone gallbladder surgery, this familiar scene might evoke a twinge of uncertainty. How does one indulge in the pleasure of baking without traditional ingredients like butter and cream, which are now off-limits due to dietary restrictions? It's a conundrum that can be as challenging as it is disheartening. But fear not—reinventing your baking repertoire to suit your new dietary needs can be both a delightful exploration and a delicious discovery.

Navigating through post-gallbladder removal means understanding how fats are digested by your body and recognizing that high-fat ingredients can lead to discomfort. Here's where our creativity in the kitchen truly shines. The world of baking without butter and cream is rich with opportunities to use alternative ingredients that align with your health requirements while still allowing you to produce sumptuous baked goods.

The journey begins with the essentials—understanding the roles that butter and cream traditionally play in baking. Butter, beyond adding flavor, provides moisture and aids in leavening. It helps in achieving that delightful crumbly texture in cookies and flakiness in pastries. Cream, on the other hand, contributes to the richness and color of baked goods. Replacing these key components involves more than swapping one ingredient for another; it demands a thoughtful approach to retain or even enhance the sensory qualities of your favorite desserts.

A starting point in this quest is exploring plant-based oils. Olive oil, for example, is a superb alternative to butter. Not only is it rich in monounsaturated fats, which are easier on your digestion, but it also adds a subtle, fruity note to dishes, which can beautifully complement ingredients like citrus and herbs. In moist cakes and bread, applesauce or mashed bananas can be used as a replacement for butter, providing the necessary binding and moisture without the heaviness of fats.

When it comes to replacing cream, the variety of available plant-based milks offers a plethora of options. Coconut milk, with its thick consistency and sweet, nutty flavor, can serve as a fantastic base for creamy desserts. Almond milk, lighter and with a more neutral taste, works well in recipes that require a thin consistency without overwhelming the flavors of other ingredients. Each alternative brings its unique profile, opening up new dimensions of taste in your baking experiments.

Another innovative replacement is the use of avocado, which, when pureed, incorporates seamlessly into recipes to provide creaminess and binding in place of butter. Its mild flavor and rich texture make it particularly effective in chocolate desserts, where it also adds a nutritional boost.

Silken tofu is another ingredient that deserves mention. It can stand in for cream in recipes like cheesecakes or creamy pies. Blended until smooth, it offers a consistency so close to that of dairy cream that you might find it hard to tell the difference, all while being lower in fat and easier for those without a gallbladder to digest.

BLUEBERRY OAT MUFFINS

PREPARATION TIME: 10 min - **COOKING TIME:** 20 min

MODE OF COOKING: Baking - **SERVINGS:** 12 muffins

INGREDIENTS:
- 1 1/2 cups rolled oats
- 1 cup whole wheat flour
- 1/2 cup applesauce (unsweetened)
- 1/2 cup almond milk
- 1/3 cup honey
- 1 tsp baking powder
- 1/2 tsp baking soda
- 1/2 tsp cinnamon
- 1/4 tsp salt
- 1 cup fresh blueberries

DIRECTIONS:
1. Preheat oven to 350°F (175°C). Line a muffin tin with paper liners.
2. In a large bowl, mix oats, flour, baking powder, baking soda, cinnamon, and salt.
3. In another bowl, combine applesauce, almond milk, and honey.
4. Add the wet ingredients to the dry ingredients and stir until just combined. Fold in the blueberries.
5. Divide the batter evenly among the muffin cups.
6. Bake for 20 minutes or until a toothpick inserted in the center comes out clean. Cool on a wire rack.

TIPS:
1. Use frozen blueberries if fresh are not available; do not thaw them before adding.
2. Add a tablespoon of chia seeds for extra fiber.
3. Store in an airtight container for up to three days or freeze for longer storage.

NUTRITIONAL VALUES: Calories: 110, Carbs: 22g, Protein: 2g, Sugar: 10g, Cholesterol: 0mg, Fat: 1.5g

ALMOND BANANA OAT COOKIES

PREPARATION TIME: 10 min - **COOKING TIME:** 15 min
MODE OF COOKING: Baking - **SERVINGS:** 12 cookies

INGREDIENTS:

- 2 ripe bananas, mashed
- 1 cup rolled oats
- 1/4 cup almond flour
- 1/4 cup unsweetened applesauce
- 1/4 cup honey
- 1 tsp vanilla extract
- 1/2 tsp cinnamon
- 1/4 tsp salt
- 1/4 cup chopped almonds

DIRECTIONS:

1. Preheat oven to 350°F (175°C). Line a baking sheet with parchment paper.
2. In a large bowl, mix mashed bananas, oats, almond flour, applesauce, honey, vanilla extract, cinnamon, and salt until well combined.
3. Fold in chopped almonds.
4. Drop spoonsful of dough onto the prepared baking sheet, flattening each slightly.
5. Bake for 15 minutes or until edges are golden brown. Cool on a wire rack.

TIPS:

1. Add 1/4 cup of dark chocolate chips for extra flavor.
2. Store cookies in an airtight container to keep them fresh.
3. Substitute chopped walnuts or pecans if desired.

NUTRITIONAL VALUES: Calories: 80, Carbs: 15g, Protein: 2g, Sugar: 7g, Cholesterol: 0mg, Fat: 2g

CHAPTER 13: THE COMPREHENSIVE 28-DAY MEAL PLAN

13.1 WEEKLY MEAL PLANS

	breakfast	snack	lunch	snack	dinner
Monday	Berry Overnight Oats	Carrot sticks with Spicy Jalapeño Hummus	Roasted Carrot and Ginger Soup	Apple slices with Almond Butter	Lemon Herb Grilled Chicken with Steamed Carrots and Honey Ginger
Tuesday	Vanilla Maple Yogurt Parfait	A small bowl of mixed berries	Spinach and Berry Delight with Lemon-Honey Dressing	Celery sticks with Roasted Red Pepper Hummus	Citrus Herb Grilled Fish with Brown Rice Pilaf with Vegetables
Wednesday	Spinach and Mushroom Egg White Omelet	A handful of almonds	Quinoa and Chickpea Salad with Lemon-Tahini Dressing	Greek yogurt with a drizzle of honey	Lemon Garlic Shrimp Pasta
Thursday	Apple Cinnamon Chia Pudding Bowl	A small apple	Mixed Greens with Cucumber and Yogurt Dill Dressing	A handful of walnuts	Hearty Chicken and Barley Soup
Friday	Creamy Buckwheat Porridge	Fresh orange slices	Farro and Roasted Vegetable Salad with Balsamic Vinaigrette	Sliced cucumber and hummus	One-Pot Lemon Herb Salmon
Saturday	Spiced Amaranth Cereal	Mango slices	Asian Chicken Lettuce Wraps	Carrot sticks with Cucumber-Dill Greek Yogurt Dip	Skillet Lemon Herb Chicken
Sunday	Berry Flaxseed Smoothie	A handful of trail mix	Lentil and Spinach Salad with Lemon Garlic Dressing	Apple slices with Creamy White Bean Spread	Broccoli and Cauliflower Casserole

WEEK 2	breakfast	snack	lunch	snack	dinner
Monday	Banana Oat Muffins	A handful of trail mix	Chicken and Vegetable Clear Broth	Sliced bell peppers with Roasted Red Pepper Hummus	One-Pot Chicken and Rice
Tuesday	Apple Cinnamon Bread	Sliced cucumbers with Spicy Black Bean Hummus	Hearty Lentil Stew	A handful of walnuts	Skillet Lemon Herb Chicken
Wednesday	Green Chia Seed Smoothie	A small bowl of mixed berries	Grilled Chicken and Quinoa Salad with Avocado Lime Dressing	Greek yogurt with a drizzle of honey	Slow Cooker Lentil Soup
Thursday	Tropical Quinoa Breakfast Bowl	Carrot sticks with Herbed Greek Yogurt Dip	Farro and Roasted Vegetable Salad with Balsamic Vinaigrette	Carrot sticks with Spicy Jalapeño Hummus	Lemon Herb Quinoa
Friday	Spinach and Avocado Green Smoothie	Apple slices with Greek Yogurt	Turkey Avocado Whole Grain Sandwich	Apple slices with Almond Butter	Spinach and Tomato Pasta
Saturday	Kale and Pineapple Green Smoothie	A handful of almonds	Spinach and Berry Delight with Lemon-Honey Dressing	A small apple	Creamy Cauliflower and Leek Soup
Sunday	Chocolate Banana Protein Shake	Celery sticks with Creamy White Bean Spread	Mixed Greens with Cucumber and Yogurt Dill Dressing	A handful of mixed nuts	Citrus Herb Grilled Fish

	breakfast	snack	lunch	snack	dinner
Monday	Vanilla Maple Yogurt Parfait	Colorful Veggie Sticks with Homemade Hummus	Grilled Chicken and Quinoa Salad with Avocado Lime Dressing	Tropical Energy Bars	Skillet Lemon Herb Chicken
Tuesday	Spiced Amaranth Cereal	Tropical Fruit Salad	Asian Chicken Lettuce Wraps	Classic Veggie Sticks with Hummus	Lemon Garlic Shrimp Pasta
Wednesday	Apple Cinnamon Chia Pudding Bowl	Roasted Red Pepper Hummus with Veggie Sticks	Mixed Greens with Cucumber and Yogurt Dill Dressing	Citrus Berry Salad	One-Pot Lemon Herb Salmon
Thursday	Green Chia Seed Smoothie	Almond Apricot Energy Bars	Farro and Roasted Vegetable Salad with Balsamic Vinaigrette	Tropical Trail Mix	Broccoli and Cauliflower Casserole
Friday	Creamy Buckwheat Porridge	Herbed Greek Yogurt Dip with Veggie Sticks	Turkey Avocado Whole Grain Sandwich	Mango Lime Sorbet	Spinach and Mushroom Quinoa Casserole
Saturday	Spinach and Mushroom Egg White Omelet	Cucumber-Dill Greek Yogurt Dip with Veggie Sticks	Tofu and Spinach Clear Broth	Classic Nuts and Fruit Trail Mix	Slow Cooker Chicken and Vegetable Stew
Sunday	Tropical Quinoa Breakfast Bowl	Spicy Jalapeño Hummus with Veggie Sticks	Lentil and Spinach Salad with Lemon Garlic Dressing	Banana Oatmeal Cookies	Mediterranean Quinoa Bowl

Week 1	breakfast	snack	lunch	snack	dinner
Monday	Berry Overnight Oats	Classic Veggie Sticks with Hummus	Chicken and Vegetable Clear Broth	Spicy Jalapeño Hummus	Slow Cooker Lentil Soup
Tuesday	Spinach and Avocado Green Smoothie	Herbed Greek Yogurt Dip with Veggie Sticks	Quinoa and Chickpea Salad with Lemon-Tahini Dressing	Tropical Trail Mix	Citrus Herb Grilled Fish
Wednesday	Banana Oat Muffins	Apple Cinnamon Muffins	Hearty Chicken and Barley Soup	Roasted Red Pepper Hummus	Hearty Lentil Stew
Thursday	Turmeric Ginger Immunity Elixir	Raspberry Lemon Sorbet	Grilled Chicken and Quinoa Salad with Avocado Lime Dressing	Mango Lime Sorbet	Chicken and Vegetable Clear Broth
Friday	Creamy Cauliflower and Leek Soup	Cucumber Mint Refresher	Lentil and Spinach Salad with Lemon Garlic Dressing	Banana Oatmeal Cookies	Broccoli and Bell Pepper Stir-Fry
Saturday	Kale and Pineapple Green Smoothie	Spicy Black Bean Hummus with Veggie Sticks	Spinach and Berry Delight with Lemon-Honey Dressing	Citrus Berry Salad	Lemon Herb Grilled Chicken
Sunday	Berry Flaxseed Smoothie	Tropical Energy Bars	Mixed Greens with Cucumber and Yogurt Dill Dressing	Classic Nuts and Fruit Trail Mix	Spinach and Mushroom Quinoa Casserole

Navigating the aisles of your local supermarket can feel like traversing a minefield, especially when you're committed to maintaining a diet that's gentle on your digestion post-gallbladder removal. As we turn the pages to the section on shopping lists, imagine stepping into the store with a plan as clear as your dietary goals—each item you pick up is a building block for your recovery and long-term well-being.

Consider this: it's Saturday morning, your shopping day. Armed with a list that's tailored to promote healing and manage your new dietary needs, you confidently bypass the temptation of processed foods that crowd the shelves, steering your cart instead towards the freshness of seasonal produce, lean proteins, and whole grains. Each item in your cart isn't just food; it's medicine, carefully selected to nourish your body without overworking your digestive system.

Here in our comprehensive guide, we simplify this process. By breaking down your weekly shopping requirements, we help ensure you're not just buying food, but making strategic choices that enhance your health. The shopping lists provided in this chapter aren't just about checking off items—it's about understanding why certain foods are pivotal and when is the best time to incorporate them into your diet.

For instance, early in your recovery, your focus might be on fibrous fruits and soothing broths, which support gentle digestion and ease your system into more complex foods. As weeks progress, the lists evolve, introducing diverse flavors and textures, ensuring your diet remains enjoyable and your palate satisfied.

By planning your shopping trips with precision, you not only save time but also eliminate the stress of last-minute decisions, which can often lead to less desirable dietary choices. This structured approach to grocery shopping reinforces the feeling of control—control over your health, your diet, and ultimately, your life post-surgery.

Let these tailored shopping lists be your companion in the journey toward a balanced diet, guiding you week by week, as you navigate the path to recovery and robust health.

Weekly Shopping Guides

Imagine setting off on your weekly grocery shopping with a sense of excitement and purpose. This isn't just any shopping trip—this is a mission to fill your kitchen with ingredients that will support your journey to digestive health and recovery. As you stroll through the aisles, your list becomes a guide, not a restriction. It's about finding joy in discovering new foods that your body will love as much as your taste buds do.

Start in the produce section, where a rainbow of colors greets you. Fresh fruits and vegetables are your best friends now, offering vitamins, minerals, and fiber to keep your digestion smooth. Look for seasonal items; not only are they often more affordable, but they also pack the most flavor. Think crisp apples in the fall, juicy berries in the summer, and hearty root vegetables in the winter.

Next, head to the grain's aisle. Whole grains like brown rice, quinoa, and oats should be staples in your pantry. They provide sustained energy and are gentle on your digestive system. Avoid overly processed grains and instead choose those that are closer to their natural state, bursting with nutrients.

The protein section is where you'll find lean options to keep your meals balanced. Skinless chicken, turkey, fish, and plant-based proteins like beans and lentils are excellent choices. They're easy to digest and versatile enough to be used in a variety of dishes. Remember, variety is key to not getting bored with your meals.

Don't forget the dairy aisle, but be mindful of what you choose. Low-fat or lactose-free options can help prevent any digestive discomfort. Greek yogurt is a great pick, rich in probiotics that support gut health.

As you move toward the end of your shopping trip, visit the spice and condiment section. Fresh herbs, spices, and low-fat dressings can transform simple ingredients into gourmet meals. Experiment with different seasonings to keep your palate excited and your meals flavorful without adding unnecessary fat.

Finally, check out the aisles with snacks and treats. Yes, you can still enjoy snacks, but opt for healthier versions. Nuts, seeds, dried fruits, and low-fat crackers are good choices. They're satisfying and nutritious, making them perfect for between meals or on-the-go munching.

Leaving the store with bags full of carefully chosen items, you'll feel prepared and empowered. Each ingredient is a step towards a healthier, more enjoyable diet, proving that shopping wisely can be both fun and rewarding.

Essential Pantry Items

Picture opening your pantry and being greeted by an array of essential ingredients, ready to create meals that nourish and comfort. A well-stocked pantry is your foundation, a reliable resource that makes cooking less daunting and more exciting.

It's not just about having ingredients on hand; it's about having the right ingredients that support your post-surgery dietary needs and inspire culinary creativity.

Imagine reaching for a jar of quinoa, knowing it's a versatile grain that provides a gentle source of protein and fiber. Nearby, cans of low-sodium beans stand ready to be transformed into hearty stews or vibrant salads. Whole grains like brown rice and oats find their place, promising sustained energy and digestive ease.

Your pantry shelves hold more than just staples; they're a treasure trove of flavors. Spices like turmeric, cumin, and ginger not only add zest to your dishes but also offer anti-inflammatory benefits. Bottles of olive oil and vinegar sit proudly, ready to dress up salads or lend depth to marinades. Herbs, whether dried or fresh, are the secret to turning simple dishes into gourmet experiences.

Let's not forget the importance of canned tomatoes and broths, the building blocks of many comforting meals. They bring convenience without compromising on flavor or nutrition. Nut butters, seeds, and dried fruits are your go-to snacks, providing healthy fats and natural sweetness.

As you stand back and admire your pantry, you realize it's more than a storage space. It's a symbol of readiness, a testament to the thought and care you've put into your dietary journey. Each item you've chosen plays a role in making mealtime not just manageable, but enjoyable and healthful. This is where your culinary adventure begins, with a pantry that promises endless possibilities.

Seasonal Ingredient Suggestions

Imagine the delight of cooking with ingredients that are not only at their peak flavor but also bring a vibrant, seasonal touch to your meals. Embracing the bounty of each season can transform your kitchen into a place of continual discovery and joy, where nature's rhythm guides your culinary choices.

In the crisp months of spring, tender asparagus, fresh peas, and sweet strawberries make their entrance. These ingredients burst with color and vitality, perfect for light salads and simple sautés that celebrate the renewal of the season. Spring greens, with their delicate leaves, add a refreshing crunch, while radishes offer a peppery kick.

As summer warms the air, the garden's bounty overflows. Think of juicy tomatoes, sweet corn, and an abundance of herbs like basil and mint. These ingredients invite you to experiment with fresh salsas, chilled soups, and vibrant salads that capture the essence of sunny days. Berries and stone fruits, like peaches and cherries, lend their natural sweetness to both savory dishes and refreshing desserts.

Autumn brings a shift to heartier fare, with root vegetables like carrots, beets, and parsnips taking center stage. Squash varieties—acorn, butternut, and pumpkin—offer a rich, comforting base for numerous dishes. Apples and pears, crisp and sweet, make their way into everything from salads to warm, spiced treats.

Winter's chill calls for ingredients that provide warmth and sustenance. Think of robust leafy greens like kale and Swiss chard, alongside winter citrus fruits like oranges and grapefruits that add a burst of brightness. Root vegetables continue to provide comfort, while nuts and seeds add depth and texture to hearty meals.

Embracing seasonal ingredients not only enhances the flavor and nutritional value of your meals but also connects you to the natural world's cycles. Each season's unique offerings bring variety and excitement, ensuring your culinary journey is as dynamic and nourishing as the changing seasons themselves.

13.3 TIPS FOR MEAL PREP AND PLANNING

Mastering the art of meal preparation is a voyage we embark on together, navigating the waters of a busy lifestyle while staying true to our dietary goals after gallbladder surgery. Picture yourself entering the kitchen on a bustling Monday morning. Everything you need for the week's meals is perfectly organized, ingredients are prepped, and your mind is clear. This isn't just a serene dream but a very achievable reality with a little forethought and some clever strategies.

Transitioning to a new dietary routine can be daunting. However, think of meal prep as your compass in the chaos—a way to anchor your eating habits and ensure you consume what is best for your body without the last-minute stress. It begins with understanding the premise that spending a couple of hours preparing at the start of the week saves precious time later. Imagine chopping vegetables for multiple meals, batch cooking grains like quinoa and rice, or marinading proteins. These are the building blocks of effortless daily cooking.

Yet, inviting efficiency into your kitchen doesn't have to mean sacrificing variety. Each week can offer a canvas for culinary experimentation within your dietary needs. Sunday might be your prep day—envision this as your time to mix flavors, organise your food, and think about the week ahead. Creating a soup could serve as a comforting lunch for several days, whereas a large salad can be tweaked with different proteins or dressings for freshness in every bite.

Strategically, think of your refrigerator and pantry as tools in your meal prep arsenal. Stocking them with essentials such as low-fat broths, lean proteins, whole grains, and vibrant produce is like keeping your toolkit filled. Moreover, segmenting cooked foods into portion-sized containers as part of your prep can make all the difference. They stand ready to be combined in various delicious, healthy meals that respect your post-surgery digestion needs.

Approach your weekly meal preparation as both a science and an art—an opportunity to nourish your body while flexing your creative culinary muscles. With every diced vegetable and every planned meal, you are stepping confidently into your week, assured that you can maintain your healthy eating habits consistently and deliciously.

Efficient Meal Prep Techniques

Imagine dedicating a quiet Sunday afternoon to transform your week through meal prep and planning. Start with a cup of tea and your favorite cookbooks, sketching out a menu that excites you and fits your schedule. Visualizing the week ahead, you can anticipate the busy evenings and leisurely mornings, aligning your meal choices with your lifestyle.

With your plan in place, create a detailed shopping list. This not only ensures you have all the ingredients but also streamlines your grocery trips. Picture the efficiency of moving through the store with purpose, avoiding the distractions and unnecessary purchases.

Back in your kitchen, the real magic happens. Begin with the basics: wash and chop your vegetables, cook grains, and portion out proteins. Imagine the satisfaction of opening your fridge to find neatly prepped ingredients, ready to be transformed into meals. This foundation makes cooking each day a breeze, reducing stress and saving precious time.

Batch cooking is a game-changer. Double your recipes for soups, stews, and casseroles, freezing half for future use. These ready-made meals are lifesavers on the busiest days, offering home-cooked nourishment with minimal effort.

Embrace flexibility. Life is unpredictable, and sometimes plans change. Keeping versatile ingredients on hand allows you to adapt, ensuring you can always whip up a delicious and healthy meal.

Time-Saving Tips

By investing a little time in meal prep and planning, you create a week of culinary ease and enjoyment. Each meal becomes a testament to your foresight and care, making healthy eating an effortless part of your daily routine.

Imagine you're in the kitchen after a long day, looking for ways to make meal prep quicker and easier. Here's where these time-saving tips come in handy. First, let's talk about batch cooking. Spend a few hours on the weekend preparing large quantities of your favorite low-fat dishes. Freeze portions in individual containers, so all you need to do on a busy night is reheat and enjoy a nutritious meal.

Next, make the most of your kitchen gadgets. A slow cooker can be a lifesaver. In the morning, toss in some lean protein, veggies, and broth, and by the time you get home, you'll have a delicious, ready-to-eat dinner. Similarly, an instant pot can reduce cooking times drastically, making it easier to whip up meals quickly.

Pre-chopped vegetables and pre-cooked grains are other great shortcuts. These can be bought at most grocery stores and save valuable prep time. Finally, keep your pantry stocked with essentials like canned beans, low-fat broths, and whole grains. Having these staples on hand means you can throw together a healthy meal without a trip to the store.

These simple strategies can transform your kitchen routine, helping you eat well without spending hours at the stove.

Adjusting the Plan to Fit Your Lifestyle

Adapting a meal plan to fit your unique lifestyle can be a game-changer in maintaining a healthy diet after gallbladder surgery. Think of your plan as a flexible guide rather than a rigid set of rules. It's about finding what works for you, whether that means adjusting meal times, incorporating family favorites, or even simplifying recipes to fit into your busy schedule.

Start by considering your daily routine. Are mornings hectic? Opt for make-ahead breakfasts that you can grab and go. If evenings are unpredictable, rely on those batch-cooked meals we discussed earlier. Tailoring your plan to your schedule ensures you're not scrambling for last-minute solutions, which often leads to unhealthy choices.

Family meals can also be a challenge, but with a bit of creativity, you can make dishes that everyone will enjoy. For instance, you can prepare a basic low-fat protein and then add different sides and seasonings to cater to varying tastes.

Remember, flexibility is key. If a planned meal doesn't appeal to you on a given day, swap it for something else that fits your dietary guidelines. The goal is to create a sustainable approach that feels natural and easy to maintain. By listening to your body and adjusting your plan accordingly, you'll find a balance that supports your health and fits seamlessly into your lifestyle.

Measurement Conversion Table

Volume Measurements

US Measurement	Metric Measurement
1 tsp (tsp)	5 milliliters (ml)
1 tbsp (tbsp)	15 milliliters (ml)
1 fluid ounce (fl oz)	30 milliliters (ml)
1 Cup	240 milliliters (ml)
1 pint (2 Cs)	470 milliliters (ml)
1 quart (4 Cs)	0.95 liters (L)
1 gallon (16 Cs)	3.8 liters (L)

Weight Measurements

US Measurement	Metric Measurement
1 ounce (oz)	28 grams (g)
1 pound (lb)	450 grams (g)
1 pound (lb)	0.45 kilograms (kg)

Length Measurements

US Measurement	Metric Measurement
1 inch (in)	2.54 centimeters (cm)
1 foot (ft)	30.48 centimeters (cm)
1 foot (ft)	0.3048 meters (m)
1 yard (yd)	0.9144 meters (m)

Temperature Conversions

Fahrenheit (°F)	Celsius (°C)
32°F	0°C
212°F	100°C
Formula: (°F - 32) x 0.5556 = °C	Formula: (°C x 1.8) + 32 = °F

Oven Temperature Conversions

US Oven Term	Fahrenheit (°F)	Celsius (°C)
Very Slow	250°F	120°C
Slow	300-325°F	150-165°C
Moderate	350-375°F	175-190°C
Moderately Hot	400°F	200°C
Hot	425-450°F	220-230°C
Very Hot	475-500°F	245-260°C

Made in the USA
Monee, IL
20 August 2024

64152301R00063